T0353672

STRANDS
OF FAITH

Conditioned by Courage, Hope and Self-Love
SHEILA YOUNG

BALBOA.PRESS
A DIVISION OF HAY HOUSE

Balboa Press books may be ordered through booksellers or by contacting:

Balboa Press
A Division of Hay House
1663 Liberty Drive
Bloomington, IN 47403
www.balboapress.com
844-682-1282

Scripture taken from the King James Version of the Bible.

Print information available on the last page.

ISBN: 979-8-7652-5910-8 (sc)
ISBN: 979-8-7652-5911-5 (hc)
ISBN: 979-8-7652-5912-2 (e)

Library of Congress Control Number: 2025900528

Balboa Press rev. date: 02/04/2025

"But the very hairs of your head are all numbered."
(Matthew 10:30)

Contents

PART THREE

*To powerful, fearless women of faith who
will carry their cross to the end*

*To prayer warriors who boldly intercede in
prayer for others and themselves*

*To that broken person in the mirror that sees
beauty, promise and freedom to live*

*To beautiful women who recognize the light she gives may
not be as bright as the light she receives in return*

*To men who love and respect their wives, and impart
wisdom and knowledge into their daughters and sons*

To all the amazing family and friends we have lost along the way

Mama Sue's Blissful Big 10

1. Get to know the Lord

2. Be known by your fruit

3. Be a lady and respect yourself

4. Embrace your own imperfections

5. Don't let your fears rule you

6. Slow down and celebrate the moments of life

7. Take care of your husband and treat him like a man

8. Be strong and realize you don't need the strict codes of cliques to feel good about yourself

9. Build a sisterhood, empower your daughters and other women in your life

10. Invest in good bras and panties

Forewords

It is an honor to introduce *Strands of Faith: Conditioned by Courage, Hope, and Self-Love* written by my friend, Sheila Young, a woman whose life and work embody resilience, faith, and creativity. Through this book, Sheila offers readers a deeply personal yet universally relevant guide to navigating life's challenges. Her reflections, grounded in scripture and fortified by life experience, invite us to trust in God's plan and embrace courage, hope, and self-love as we move through life's seasons.

Sheila has been a part of my life for many years through her close friendship with my mom. Over time, she has become much more than a family friend—she's someone whose wisdom and creativity I deeply admire. Sheila's thoughtful touch has elevated some of my life's most meaningful moments, including my wedding and my mom's sixtieth birthday. As a fine artist and designer, I am inspired by Sheila's ability to transform everyday events into unforgettable experiences, always infused with heart and intention.

Her professional journey is as inspiring as the lessons she shares in this book. Her common strand has always been people—building meaningful connections and empowering others to reach their full potential.

In *Strands of Faith*, Sheila shares the wisdom she has gained from navigating life's challenges, including those uniquely shaped by her experience as a Black woman. Through this lens, she offers profound insights into overcoming adversity, embracing strength, and trusting in God's plan. Chapters like "My Black 6.2" and "Workplace Wisdom" reveal how Sheila has turned obstacles into stepping stones for personal and spiritual growth, offering powerful lessons for anyone who seeks to rise above life's challenges.

What makes this book so special is Sheila's ability to blend her life experiences with wisdom that feels both practical and profound. Each story is like a carefully chosen thread in a tapestry, woven together to create something strong, beautiful, and deeply meaningful. Through themes such as "Prayer is a Lifestyle" and "God Knows the Story Behind Your Tears," Sheila reminds us that faith is both a source of strength and a tool for transformation.

As you read *Strands of Faith: Conditioned by Courage, Hope, and Self-Love*, allow Sheila's words to encourage and uplift you. Her stories serve as a reminder that no matter the challenges we face, faith and perseverance can carry us through. Sheila's insights are not just lessons—they are gifts of encouragement meant to inspire action, self-reflection, and trust in the extraordinary plans God has for your life.

Prepare to be moved, strengthened, and reminded of the beauty of God's grace. This is more than a book; it's a companion for life's journey, offering the wisdom and hope we all need to keep moving forward in faith.

~ Ali Hall, Fine Artist and Designer

If you are looking to be set up for a great comeback from any and all setbacks, look no further. You've found it! Hi all, Kimmiko here! I am an avid reader and author. I have been given the honor of writing a foreword for, *Strands of Faith: Conditioned by Courage, Hope and Self-Love.* I must admit when I was first asked to write this, I was, of course, humbled, and also a little shocked: even though I have known Sheila for many years (yes many, we actually go back all the way to the 1980s). Sheila and I both love the Lord, family, and all things beauty. Our strongest bond, I believe, may be that we are hard core encouragers of women–we want us to win.

Even with all that in mind, I still thought *Why me, Lord?* I now know why: receiving an advance copy was my own personal set-up for a comeback. So first, and foremost, I give God all the glory and say *thank you* to my dear friend for answering the charge to write this amazing book! Lives will be transformed.

In *Strands of Faith*, you will find places where you may want to get your highlighter out, read a sentence aloud, or make some sort of declaration or affirmation for the day. It may be for any or all projects you have ahead of you. Sheila's transparency allows you to be honest with yourself, about yourself. On the following pages you will see you are not alone, and even if you are going through it at this very moment, you can and will be okay. God's got you!

The way I see it, *Strands of Faith* is broken down into three parts: Gratitude, Forgiveness, and Seasons. Be sure to pay attention to each and every nugget. On these pages a light will come on that you didn't know had been dimmed–there is nothing like an "ah-ha" moment. All of us are faced with fiery trials, and sometimes we go on autopilot– just keep going and going. We forget there are times in life when we are not okay and that it's okay to feel that way. This book will help all who need to stop and smell the roses, take that break, get back to praying, and meditate on what is true, lovely, sound, a good report, or praiseworthy. It is time to find that thing that truly brings you joy! And remember this: *self-love is not selfish; the devil is a liar!*

What are you looking for? Is it encouragement, maybe some workplace wisdom, a little marriage spice? Could it be you're dealing with heartbreak, or going through a custody battle? Or is it unforgiveness? I am telling you now, beloved, you will find it all in *Strands of Faith*! As the saying goes, *she left no crumbs*. There are times when I read this book where I felt Sheila cheering me on. You will feel that too–her encouragement jumps off the pages.

It's time now for you to dive in. Grab a highlighter, maybe a notebook. Pour yourself some tea, a cup of coffee or a glass of Malbec–the choice is yours. Happy reading!

~ *Kimberly "Kimmiko" Keeton*

Introduction

Do you find it challenging to support yourself in difficult times? When you face your deepest fears, your most painful moments, the most unimaginable despair, do you trust God to do the impossible? Where do you find power strong enough to make it through the storms of life? Could it be that believing in God's power to help discover our faith serves as a foundation for our courage, hope and self-love?

Faith, while it can be difficult to practice, is your most powerful weapon to conquer and attain anything. That which seems impossible becomes possible through prayer and faith in God.

This book is a collection of the inspiring and faith-affirming personal insights I learned during years of transformation and finding myself through courage, hope, and self-love in the Strands of Life. Each section has a powerful Strand story full of emotion, challenge, heartbreaking failures, survival, discovery, gratitude, and promise in day-to-day living. These stories are designed to teach you the ways God can renew our minds and bring us peace—building the muscles to celebrate life and God's love when it seems you have nothing to celebrate at all. It is deliberate with purposeful testimonies of how I gained wisdom, strength, knowledge, and fortitude by trusting and having faith in the Creator—believing His strength is made perfect in my weakness.

Strands of Faith is not a memoir. It is a sweet piece of faith I pray will speak to your spirit in the right way at the right time–finding feelings of joy in the moment of each Strand. I have written this book in sections, each featuring a stimulating biblical power verse and a powerful inspirational quote from women I admire. Each section is a gift of encouragement for believers, prayer warriors, and soldiers on the battlefield. It is a "pick-me-up" for those who are curious, or just stepping into a relationship with God. At the end, you will find a Strands *Play It Loud* playlist QR code. My suggestion is that you play it loud and let the music vibrate through your body and move you!

The basis of living our best life beyond our imagination comes from knowing who is in control and knowing what is important in life. God tells us what is important in His word, which does not return void. The feelings we experience each day, such as brokenness, wholeness, doubt, fear, anger, and happiness, can be from our outlook rather than our circumstances. We all have the power to choose to walk in faith instead of sight.

God has something magical He wants to do in your life. Trust Him. Pray and speak faith into your future. Sometimes it feels like God doesn't hear you or God has let you down. Know that God hears you even when you can't hear yourself. He is always working things out for your good. Resolve to let faith be your first response when life threatens to overwhelm you. My prayer is that by the time you get to the end of Strands of Faith, a spark is ignited that moves your soul in a greater sense of direction and meaning for your own beautiful narrative.

Take note: You may find yourself experiencing more joy and taking on new opportunities. Don't be surprised if others around you start having the same experiences.

Count your blessings! The best thing about Faith, Courage, Hope and Self-Love is they are free! Let possibility flow from your mind, heart, and being. It's never too late to live your wildest dreams.

PART ONE

"NOW FAITH is the substance of things hoped for, the evidence of things not seen."
(Hebrews 11:1)

PART ONE

Gratitude

"In everything give thanks: for this is the will
of God in Christ Jesus concerning you."
(1 Thessalonians 5:18)

"Gratitude will give you strength for the joy and
peace in your heart to burst into flames."
~ Mama Sue

A t a young age, I promoted myself and assumed the role of
the eldest of three siblings; much like Thelma Evans from
the sitcom Good Times. I am the middle child of four, between
an older brother, and a younger sister and brother. For the most
part, my sister and brothers were easygoing and didn't require
much. They embraced the spirit of gratitude at an early age. I
was my mom and dad's right hand, even when they didn't need
me to be. I positioned myself as the bonus parent, where I called
the shots and made the rules. I embraced my makeshift role very
well, or at least I did in my mind

I have always enjoyed giving. Anytime I am able to bless someone
with a trinket–it is on! However, I still hadn't learned how to receive
with gratitude. I was an ungrateful, demanding, unappreciative
human with lots of ambition mixed with an excessive sense of self-
importance and high expectations. I expected others to give to me

1

the way I wanted. My pathetic attitude was, *if you can't give me what I ask for, don't get me anything at all.* My ungrateful behavior would often leave my family and friends walking on eggshells.

One year, I received a candle from a friend for my birthday. Without any consideration of the potential financial sacrifice or emotional intention behind her gift, I returned it. I didn't feel it was comparable to what I would have given her and it just didn't meet my standards. It was all about me! My high expectations made my friends very uncomfortable; they couldn't understand how I could be such a giver yet so ungrateful and unappreciative.

"It is more blessed to give than receive." (Acts 20:35)

I had a "bless the receiver" attitude. I was clueless about being grateful in all things. I misinterpreted the meaning of that verse and lived with a twisted version of it for years.

The Christmas before my fifteenth birthday I got a rude awakening. I had prayed to God for a pair of black boots. One day, my mom took me to Emporium Capwell to show her the exact pair I wanted to be strutting in. She was surprised at how much the boots cost, as well as the nerve I had asking for high-priced boots they couldn't afford. They had three other children to purchase gifts for. I don't remember if I had any consideration of what was going on in my mom's mind, but if I did, I didn't care. I wanted those boots.

Leading up to Christmas day, I was excited to see my gifts under the tree, particularly the gift wrapped in the same shape and size as a boot box. I went as far as making a special place in my closet to display my boots. I was ready. On Christmas day we unwrapped our gifts and I saved the boot box for last. I peeled the wrapping paper off slowly, while thanking my mom and dad, in advance, for granting my wish. My sister sat smiling as she watched me. When I opened the box a frilly, blue, Jessica McClintock robe fell from the tissue paper. I actually thought it was a prank at first. Then reality settled in. I was devastated.

As the tears fell from my eyes, I asked: "Why did you do this to me? Where are my boots?"

I left the frilly, blue robe in the box and stormed to my room. I cried myself to sleep while my family continued on enjoying Christmas. I had a chip on my shoulder for days, which my parents did not entertain.

My breakthrough happened when my mom and dad had enough of my nonsense. They refused to let my ungrateful attitude go on any longer. While we had many conversations about gratitude which, by the way, went in one ear and out the other, this particular time felt different. Mom had me take a look at myself. She presented examples of how I was showing up and how I was making others feel. It was so embarrassing hearing it all played back to me. I felt horrible. My mom was fed up, but she went on to share suggestions on how to deal with my lack of empathy for others.

The moral of her story: Focus on being grateful for what God had blessed me with rather than what I thought I needed or didn't have. No matter what, accept the gift whether you want it or not. All you need to say are two words: **Thank You.**

My mom also told me being ungrateful had consequences. I could miss out on the special, unimaginable blessings God had in store for me. She took out her yellow legal pad and had me write down things I was grateful for each day. She had unlocked the truth in the emotions I was carrying around, particularly as it related to my sense of entitlement. Simply said, she reminded me no one owes me anything. These powerful conversations went on for weeks. While I was still a work in progress, I began making gratitude a priority, and it started to show. My inner circle became less tense around me and the tension in my house began to dissipate. Fast forward years later, I am still a giver *and* gratitude now flows authentically from my heart. Oh, and "the boots meltdown" has been a favorite joke at every family gathering ever since.

On April 13, 2024, I had an amazing lunch with my "returned candle" friend. We have remained close over the years, and our gut wrenching laughter and conversations have always been food for my soul. On this day, I found the perfect moment to ask for her forgiveness for returning her candle gift. She actually remembered the moment and blurted out, "Really, Sheila?"

We both laughed, and she said, "Good Lord, you sure have come a long way, my friend."

While we tried to remember the year it happened and the scent of the candle, she said, "It is never too late to forgive."

Nodding my head in agreement, I replied, "We are all a work in progress, and it's never too late to make changes in your life to become a better person."

One thing I know for sure, you can never recreate the exact same moments you are in; therefore be grateful for all of them.

WAKE UP AND GIVE GOD ALL THE PRAISE, HONOR, AND GLORY!

Imagine waking up everyday with an attitude of gratitude. No matter what your morning routine is, starting your day with praise and gratitude is a great way to wake up. When you wake up feeling grateful, you honor the life you have, and you open your heart to experience the fullness of joy throughout the day. We all have the power to choose an attitude of gratitude.

As you go about your day, look around at all the things and people that cross your path. Pay attention to the things that bring you joy and give thanks for them showing up in your life. Gratitude is a mindset of focusing on opportunity and fullness, rather than negativity and defeat. Start where you are and be honest about your feelings.

It is important to get in the routine of making time for gratitude, particularly when those out of body experiences hit. It can be as simple as giving yourself time to step away for a moment. Perhaps go for a quick walk or step outside for a breath of fresh air. The separation from the situation can be enough to help you to reset your thinking and get you back in your body.

Be a cheerful giver. I love giving and making others happy. It makes me feel great. It took me time to learn that letting others make me happy is just as amazing as giving. I now know that giving expresses a heart of gratitude in passing along a portion of the blessings we receive. Find a way to give unconditionally, trusting God will provide the same as you do. Be grateful in everything, become an appreciator of everything big and small. While being grateful to others, remember to be grateful to yourself!

Prayer Is A Lifestyle

"After this manner therefore pray ye: Our Father which art in heaven. Hallowed be thy name. Thy kingdom come. Thy will be done on earth, as it is in heaven. Give us this day our daily bread. And forgive us our debts, as we forgive our debtors. And lead us not into temptation, but deliver us from evil: For thine is the kingdom, and the power, and the glory, for ever. Amen."
(Matthew 6:9-13)

"You can pray until you faint, but unless you get up and try to do something, God is not going to put it in your lap."
~ Fannie Lou Hamer

God wants us to praise and give Him glory often. Attending church as a family was a top priority for my parents. It was our time to push aside all distractions to praise and worship God. It strengthened our family bond, as well as our individual faiths. Our parents believed worshiping together gave us guidance on how to follow God, that it created a foundation for us to serve beyond ourselves. We were all very active in church and involved in several ministries. Our social life revolved around church. Sundays were long. Through it all Mom had a solid, structured routine, while Dad prepared a delicious, hot breakfast every morning. Mom and Dad churched us out! Our Sundays started with Sunday school, followed by 11:00 a.m. service, sometimes followed by a potluck after church, going home for a few hours to eat dinner, and returning to church for revival services at 6:00 p.m. Oftentimes we were in church three to five days a week without a choice in the matter. The plan was simple: no church, no going out with friends. And don't even think about pulling out the "I'm sick" card.

The comedy often started on Sunday mornings before church–Dad calm, Mom in complete multi-tasking mode, while us kids argued over who would use the bathroom first and who would set the table. Things like shoes were forgotten and we would have to make a U-turn back to the house. Some would complain about a stomachache all the way to church, while others threw temper tantrums. The list of distractions was endless.

Thank you Jesus! Once we entered the doors of the church, we put on our happy faces, received our programs, and hummed *Yes, Jesus loves me*, while making our way to our seats. Now, if someone was sitting in our seats it prompted a whole other type of chaos. We were notorious for claiming unofficial ownership of our seats, yet we also understood we were there to serve and regardless of where we sat we would still be fed the Word.

As I got older and understood the Word, I realized the devil was trying to wreak havoc in our household to keep us from church and praising the Lord, but the devil is a liar. To this day, I am strengthened when I am around other believers, hearing their testimonies, and seeing their faith.

Family prayer life was as important as attending church. It helped instill a sense of reverence, gratitude and humility in me. As I got older, I learned prayer is as important to my spiritual life as breathing is to my physical being.

PRAYER IS A CONVERSATION

Prayer is the soul of a Believer's relationship with God. When we pray, we are inviting God into our lives. It gives us direct connection, allowing us to build a relationship with Him. It is how we speak to Him. It is how we hear Him. It is how we develop an emotional relationship with Him. Just like any relationship, you have to do your part. God expects us to act boldly. He wants us to trust His "yes," "no" or "delay" messages. No matter what answers God gives, He knows what we need before we ask, and when we need it, even if it may not be on our timing.

Prayer builds our faith. God answers our prayers in the form of thoughts, spiritual feelings, scriptures, and the actions of others. Be patient, allow the waiting period to grow your faith and trust in God. Make certain that He, and He alone, receives all the glory, praise, and honor for pulling you through. It is important to pray in times of joy and in times of heaviness. Pray until something happens. Pray for yourself and others, including the ones who have been hurtful, harmful or hateful to you–especially for them. Praying for people who hurt you is really, really, really hard, but I speak from experience when I say that it not only frees you from resentment, it brings you peace and comfort. Simply pray by asking God to forgive them in hopes that God may change their hearts too.

PRAYER HAS POWER!
WHEN PRAYERS GO UP, BLESSINGS COME DOWN!

"Ye ask, and receive not, because you ask amiss."
(James 4:3)

When you pray for something, be ready to deal with everything that comes with it. You may go through difficulties before you

8

get a breakthrough. It is important to be specific in your prayer. If you want God to bless you with a new car, ask specifically for what you want. I mean extremely specific. Let's say you pray for a car and God blesses you with a 1995 Honda Accord. You are upset because you were hoping for a brand new Mercedes Benz. Why? You asked God for a car and He blessed you with one. The problem could be the request did not include the details such as make, model, color, interior, exterior, affordable payments, reliability, heated seats, etc. Or it could be you are not taking care of the car you currently own. You get the point.

Even though God knows what you need even before you ask, He loves to hear from you while He is on His search. God expects us to be good stewards of what we have so he can advance you to the next level of wheels. Continue to be grateful for every big and little thing you receive. God always makes a way!

Worthy Wise Counsel

*"Where no counsel is, the people fall: but in the
multitude of counsellors there is safety."*
(Proverbs 11:14)

*"Invest in the human soul, who knows, it
may be a diamond in the rough."*
~ Mary McLeod Bethume

S ometimes all you need is a bit of reassurance to remember
that you are strong, confident, and worth it. My Worthy
Wise Counsel does that for me. They are truly a force to be
reckoned with.

My drive and hustle comes from my mother and father. They
were my first go-to wise counsel, and continue to be my number
one support system. They have guided me through personal and
professional challenges by pouring out wisdom and knowledge that
helped shape my life. They have supported me unconditionally
through my highs and lows. They've had the greatest influence
on me. They set the fire in me and allowed me to dream without
limits. I thank them every chance I get for nurturing what God
gave me.

DIVA MAMAS

On the job, in the family, church, community, and with friends, my mom touched and inspired the hearts of many without judgment. She loves unconditionally. She is always true to her word, very courageous and faces her fears head on. It is not often that I've seen her sweat. Not only is she a great mom, she has always been a role model worthy of imitating my entire life, and continues to be a reliable source of wisdom in my life to this day. We have become buddies over the years, enjoying the excitement of traveling and discovering unfamiliar places together–checking off her bucket list one vacation at a time.

In the late 1980s, my mom transferred to Philadelphia to continue her amazing career, knowing she left me and my siblings in good hands. While her phone line was available 24/7, it was comforting to know I had, and still have, a community of wise counsel to turn to during difficult times. I call them my "DIVA Mamas." *DIVA defined: Divinely Inspired Virtuously Accelerated.* (May you continue to rest in heavenly peace Diva Mamas: BS, SD and AH).

All my DIVA Mamas, who happened to be my mom's best friends, took me under their wings at a very young age. They are prayer warriors and have prayed over me in every direction. They help me see hope in myself. They have a proven track record of making good judgments based on their experiences–the falls and wins in their own lives–and help me get through similar situations in my life.

There have been many times when I have reached out for help: From pulling me out from under the blanket after a breakup, to driving me to college orientation, to coming over in the middle of the night to give me pointers on how to get a good latch when I was breastfeeding.

Most were very sensitive about embarrassing topics when I was brave enough to ask for help. Soon I realized I wasn't alone and needed to speak up. While I have the answers to many things, I am grateful I have the wisdom of knowing I don't know everything. I am in good hands and they help me in my journey.

FROM DAD TO BEST FRIEND

With my dad, making the transition from daughter to best friend was a seamless process. Growing up Pops was clear that his role as a father was to be a parent first. He made his boundaries very clear and did not blur the lines of his authority and responsibility. This gave me the opportunity to learn and test my emotions and appropriate behavior in the safe space of our home, rather than on the playground. The way he counseled me then was from a father's perspective, today he inspires me as a trusted friend. At eighty-nine he still praises all us children and often states that we are the air he breathes, which always makes my heart smile.

GOD SENDS THE PEOPLE YOU NEED

When you need that extra push, feel anxious, frustrated or sad, trust you are not alone. God sends people into our lives to heal, support and comfort us. Lean into the people who have lived in ways that inspire you and will share their life experiences and wisdoms with you. Develop trust in these relationships. Let your circle of wise counsel support and help you by being in the moment with you. Most likely they have been there, done that!

Be sure to express your appreciation to the people who have poured greatness into your life. Let them know you are grateful and that you care by making time to visit them, sending a letter or chatting with them on the phone. Keep the memories alive and remind them by sharing a specific example of something they did for you and how it made a difference in your life.

EMBRACING MY TURN TO
EXCITE AND ENERGIZE

Now that I am older and wiser, I have realized it's my turn to become Worthy Wise Counsel to those inside and outside of my circle. It is my time to excite and energize others with joy. It is with gratitude that I am called upon to help others find meaning and purpose in whatever that "thing" may be for them. I carry the torch and wear my badge of honor proudly, just like my Worthy Wise Counsel did for me. Part of being Worthy Wise Counsel is honoring what people tell you, no matter the magnitude of their situation, with due regard and confidentiality.

I am known for sharing practical advice and inspiration based on my own wins and falls, while pointing to the Word for spiritual enlightenment. I listen to what is being said while paying attention to the unspoken word, which often speaks louder. Sometimes the crucial conversations can get heated with emotions running strong, but the number one goal is to energize them to move forward while strutting with resilience and determination. It's all in the spirit of trust, mutual respect and love. Bridging truth to power!

When We Fumble
And Fall, We Rise

"Rejoicing in hope; patient in tribulation;
continuing instant in prayer;"
(Romans 12:12)

"There is no such thing as failure. Failure is just
life trying to move us in another direction."
~ Oprah Winfrey

After searching for employment online, I found the dream job with my name on it at a startup company. I pressed submit and applied for the job. While the job market was very competitive, I was confident in my portfolio and knew I would get the job. I met all of the requirements with a very motivational mindset. I was prepared to talk about myself and past positions. Having worked in staffing, I understood people hire people.

To my surprise a few weeks later I received a *thank you, but no thank you* rejection email. I followed up with the human resources department to get feedback but never heard back. I didn't let the rejection hinder my confidence though and applied for another position at the same company–checking my motivation for reapplying, asking myself *Am I trying to prove a point or am I really interested in working for the company?* I determined I was still committed to going through the process. The next interview went very well and I was sure I got the position. Well, I received another rejection letter–strike two. I continued to apply for other roles only to receive more rejections or no responses at all.

I felt like a failure, particularly since my peers were landing jobs with great benefit packages. The rejections triggered a range of emotions including frustration, sadness, hurt feelings, and self-doubt. It took me time to move forward. As I reflected on my strengths, accomplishments, and what's up for me next, I was reminded that rejection is a part of life. I began to think about the bigger picture and didn't let this hinder my motivation and drive. I am a firm believer that God does not make mistakes. The start-up company only lasted a few years. I eventually stepped out on faith and landed a rewarding, fun job that paid $15.00 an hour. I had to sacrifice and pause a lot of my wants to pay the bills. My friends thought I was crazy, but I had a bigger goal in mind. I learned what I needed to learn while having an amazing time along the journey. Within three years I was back to the six-digit income I was accustomed to earning. Perhaps things worked out as they were supposed to–God works in mysterious ways. Sometimes we have to change the course, but first we have to put our trust in Him.

FAILURES HELP US RISE

When we fumble and fall we learn valuable lessons as we rise. It is impossible to live without failing at something. Failure is not about who we are and where we are, it's about where we're going. Experiencing failure can be devastating and feel like the end of the world, but setbacks are a part of life. It's how we navigate through them that sets us up for growth. Our emotions can run rampant when we fall–it's absolutely normal to feel disappointed and frustrated during this time.

Take time to dust yourself off. Face the reality of your situation. Reflect, own and process the situation. Be kind to yourself and learn what you need to learn. Focus on things you can control. Love yourself just as much as when you win. Don't isolate yourself. Unlock your energy from within. Seek inspiration from your community of Worthy Wise Counsel. Ask for their advice and learn about their experiences and paths of overcoming failure. Gain knowledge from their struggles and achievements, and apply strategies to your situation where appropriate. Keep your friends and wise counsel on speed dial should you need them.

BEWARE: YOU WILL FIND OUT WHO YOUR TRUE FRIENDS ARE DURING THIS TIME

As odd as it may seem, some people will use your failures to feel better about themselves. Sometimes they don't want you to succeed. They delight in the negative spotlight of others. This has nothing to do with you–they are envious of your gifts. Count on those who love and encourage you. Your true friends will not stand in judgment. They will be there for you as long as you need them.

Believe in yourself and embrace a new approach. When we keep doing the same thing, we get the same frustrating results. Break free from this cycle and unleash the power of unlimited possibilities. Stay inspired by your past accomplishments and strengths. Keep learning and moving forward.

Failure is when we refuse to rise and try again. Wisdom comes from failure. God transforms us through these experiences if we allow Him to do so. Your story is still being written. Keep going and lean into your faith. The best is yet to come! Remember failure is a temporary condition, we rise by embracing the journey towards success.

Make Your Limits Unquestionably Clear

"But let your communication be, yea, yea, nay, nay:..."
(Matthew 5:37)

"I'm sick and tired of being sick and tired."
~ *Fannie Lou Hamer*

There have been many times in my life where I have sacrificed my own needs for others, taking on more than my share of responsibilities, leaving me feeling overwhelmed, stressed, and exhausted. I would tell myself *this is the last time* but before I knew it I was repeating the same enabling behavior and getting played over and over again. I kept giving my heart, my mind, and my money; making bad investments with no return. Man, it took a toll. Not only was my enabling behavior crippling me, it was causing damage to my relationships.

It was hard for me to reconcile how I kept allowing the cycle to continue–sitting on the sidelines while the faultfinders, who stood in judgment of me, cast blame and threw shade. It was frustrating, particularly because these naysayers weren't content with their own situations. I often found myself shutting them down with scriptures like Matthew 7:3: "Why beholdest thou the mote that is in thy brother's eye, but considerest not the beam in thine own eye."

I remember praying sun up to sun down. Praying for the situations and praying for the faultfinders. Praying for patience and understanding. Slowly, I began to realize their situations were beyond my control and that I had a difficult time letting go because my biggest fear was no one would step up and help them. I thought *I* was the remedy to their problems. Eventually I got fed up with bandaging everything. It was time to draw my own line in the sand and let go of the self-imposed responsibility. And you know what happened when I let go? The world did not come to an end!

In an effort to create a balanced life that promoted overall health and happiness, I committed to protecting my energy. After several failed attempts, I learned *my life* was more important than trying to solve problems that weren't mine to solve.

PROTECT YOURSELF

It is important to empower ourselves to create guidelines of how we want to be treated and setting clear boundaries. To give ourselves permission to let others know what is and is not okay. It's a form of self-care that honors our need to feel respected and safe and to thrive in our daily lives.

Caution! Defining our boundaries is often met with criticism and conflict by others because of their need to keep things status quo, to be right, and/or to maintain control of the narrative. When this happens, remember taking care of yourself, regardless of what other people think, is the right thing to do. We run the risk of being taken advantage of when we don't set boundaries.

Make your boundaries unquestionably clear. Determine what's important to you, focusing on *your* unique needs and wants. Recognize you deserve to be treated with respect. Boundaries may vary for each relationship. What is okay for some, may not be okay for others.

FAMILY SHENANIGANS CAN GET INTERESTING

I love my family regardless if they are good, bad, right, wrong or detached. I love them all. Huge hearts, good intentions paired with a great deal of control issues can sometimes cause us to get in our own way though; get us caught up in our own egos. Our views can change over time–no right or wrong here–we simply view the same thing differently. Love and laughter, which was once the glue that held your family together growing up, may look different when you get older and as the individual families grow.

Gatherings can get complicated, exhausting and awkward. The sandbox feels different. Laughter becomes replaced with division, drama and dysfunction. Reconciliation becomes difficult. You do all you can to celebrate the moments together, but you find yourself defending an old worn out story from the past that has been twisted over time. It is impossible to repair any wounds or broken promises from the past. You feel the tension of the coarse brown sand of delusion and chaos sprouting its ugly head. What happened to sharing a great time with great people with the common goal to build, uplift and inspire each other?

If you alone refuse to deal with your own issues, how can you expect your tribe to deal with them for you? That has always puzzled me. Sometimes chaos is what we need to make a change. You fight to salvage what's left in the relationships until you unfortunately realize you have no more fight left in you. Cherish the moments you spend with them and continue to love them from a distance. I've learned to take the high road with my family, particularly to protect my awesome and aging parents from getting caught up in the middle of the conflict. The less burden they have to bear of trying to glue the shattered pieces of their grown children together, their quality of life will be better.

Not wanting to play in the sandbox under those conditions doesn't mean you don't love them anymore. What it does mean is that you love yourself more. Our boundaries are our safety zones that keep us guarded from drama. Making your boundaries unquestionably clear brings peace of mind and gives you a sense of control over how you spend your time. Keep praying and keep your foot on the pedal. You've got this!

Workplace Wisdom

"Wisdom is the principal thing; therefore get wisdom:
and with all thy getting get understanding."
(Proverbs 4:7)

"If they don't give you a seat at the
table, bring your folding chair."
~ *Shirley Chisholm*

My mom, my SHEro, vivacious, the classiest, best mother ever! My superhero who somehow did everything. I am grateful for all of her sacrifices and hard work. She has always been an amazing trailblazer and hard worker who thrived gracefully in male-dominated Fortune 500 companies. She taught me to work hard, play harder, and, while you're at it, pull your dress down in the back. She impressed upon me the need to be self-sufficient, to invest, and plan for the future.

My dad, my HEro, the coolest, calmest, and wisest man I know. He taught me the importance of education, the essentials of business, and how to navigate the corporate world with professionalism. He drilled the importance of gaining understanding in all things while staying situationally aware. His message was very clear: **stand up for who you are as a person.**

I've been blessed with a rewarding career journey; one I wouldn't change for the world. I found meaning and purpose in every job. I have had many great memories, growth opportunities, valuable connections and intellectual stimulation. I had the opportunity to work on several multi-disciplinary teams. My career highlights included global recruitment, guest experience, training and development, project managing 600,000 square-foot flagship hospitals and parking structures, banking, transportation systems management, event planning, style coaching, cosmetology and tons of community service. The common thread throughout my career was people–making connections specifically. And I was great at it. Customers became close friends that I still have to this day.

Nevertheless, for every strong connection made, there were many forced relationships with insecure, mean people, or snooty couples who carried a sense of entitlement on their shoulders. It was a lot to handle, yet I was always up for the challenge. I was perceived as a trusted and positive person whose great energy made others feel safe, happy, and inspired. This is my truth. I acknowledge that I have a gift for bringing an energy that inspires people and gravitates them to me. And I have used this gift to my advantage throughout my career.

In every role I held, I was determined to exceed expectations. My goal was to authentically represent myself, the company, and the community. I was always humble and hungry to learn. My performance reviews were consistently stellar. I learned valuable lessons and excelled in my various roles.

For most of my career I was one of the few Black women in a leadership role and was often the company's sole representation for the entire race. However, I did not let that slow me down. I was often accused of being an Uncle Tom, or told things like, *you only got this job, because the company had to meet the EEO quota* or *what did you do to get this job?*

It was absolutely disgusting to hear, especially because some of the loudest voices were "friends" who were also Black. They made these comments without consideration of my skills, qualifications, or my hard-earned degree in business management. That truly hurt my heart, but I didn't allow their actions to derail my career strut because my true squad knew the real deal. Ching Ching! Sadly, for many women, everyone is competition, even so-called friends and coworkers who are trying to mask their own insecurities.

One of the stops on my career journey was one for the books. It was the year of the smoke, to say the least. I was isolated and lacked allies. During this season I encountered daunting obstacles, including navigating unrealistic expectations, gaslighting, macroaggressions, blatant ridicule, and racism. The old boys club had taken over, women were an afterthought–if you were a Black woman you did not exist in their minds at all. It came to a point where it felt as if the organization had no real use for Black people unless there was a need for their lifestyle marketing photography–my Black hands and blurred out Black face became very important to them then.

I recall one incident as if it were yesterday. A team of us were in an online quarterly budget meeting when a coworker openly stated, "The organization should set a spending limit for Black people as their dollar spend is much less than our white clients."

I nearly fell off my seat. I immediately challenged her, asking, "What exactly do you mean?"

Of course she tried to clean it up, only making the situation worse. Everyone else on the call, who happened to be white, either turned off their cameras or muted themselves. I questioned everyone and all they could do was stare awkwardly back at me.

I had to take a pause from the pain and plan my next move. I knew I needed to stand up for myself, and I went about methodically planning my next steps. After meeting with my director and gathering my facts, I filed an official complaint with human resources. When the "Human Resources Business Partner" (who also happened to be a white woman) reviewed my complaint, she looked at me sideways; as though I were the one who violated their so-called DEI program. I did not let her behavior interfere with my plan. I continued to stand up for myself and those who would come after me. I stuck to the truth that manifested in me during this experience. My complaint was eventually substantiated because there were witnesses who stood up to validate my experience. This "victory" was tinged however by the many so-called "work buddies" who refused to be involved in the process claiming they "couldn't remember the details." Troubling to say the least!

There was a time when I thoroughly enjoyed this job, but it had become crystal clear to me that the season had ended. The company's brand of obliviousness and self-absorbed egos wore me down. There was too much heaviness in my spirit, my strut had become a limp, and going to work had become a chore. I came to the realization that their narrative of lies, deceit, and unfair treatment were not going to change and I refused to mask who I was or accept it. I knew it was time to move on—time to lock the door, turn in the keys and never look back! I knew that my steps were ordered by the Lord and I was excited about the next chapter.

FUEL FOR THE JOURNEY

The workplace can be a challenging environment, especially for women. We often face systemic barriers that hinder our career progression and limit our opportunities for advancement. These barriers include discrimination, unconscious bias, pay disparity, and an overall lack of equal opportunity. Navigating through assumptions made about women, particularly women of color, is challenging and difficult to overcome. The way we speak, the way we dress, our race, and age are often discounted, undermined, and, in some cases, used against us. It can dim our light and deflate our ambition to be unstoppable. That's why it's extremely important for us to take an active role in our experiences–to make the time to understand an organization's human resource policies, particularly its diversity and inclusivity program. We need to know the people behind the scenes, especially those who don't look like us. It is our obligation to participate in the training and conversations that are happening around us. Hold your company accountable. Gather a diverse group of individuals together to bring a new perspective of innovation and connectivity to the company and broaden the cultural mindset.

Every individual has his/her own unique sense of self and different diversity experiences that are important to share. The lack of this knowledge can lead to misunderstandings and missed opportunities for support and protection in the workplace. The key takeaway here is this: **In order to build stronger and more equitable workplaces staff at *all levels* must be empowered to be a part of the solution**. Your story and experiences empower and inspire others and ultimately lead to a more diversified and enjoyable workplace. Believe in yourself and own your voice. How you show up will make a difference in your work day, as well as your personal life. You don't need everybody to be for you, you just need the right people to stand by you.

YOUR ULTIMATE POWER SOURCE

There is only one you and that is your ultimate power source! Believing in yourself means having faith in your own capabilities.

Your voice matters, you earned your seat at the table regardless of what they may think. It's up to you to wear your hard hat to the table and come to eat. Speak greatness about yourself and own your responsibility to help others see your value. Putting yourself out there can be frightening but I encourage you to move beyond the fear because what you have to offer is needed. Stepping out of your wheelhouse is a sure way to get noticed. You have a choice to stand out or blend into the workplace. When you step up and stand out others see your uniqueness as your strength and it sets you apart from everyone else. You deserve the blessings that God has in store for you. Bet on yourself. Set your goal, invest in yourself, and learn what you need to learn. Take calculated risks and welcome new challenges. Know your power and strength. Don't let anyone limit your access to your power. You matter. Work for it and grow from it. No dream is too big to attain!

OFFICE FAITH

Keep the faith! You are your priority. Stay true to yourself and don't change who you are to fit in at work. Sharing your faith in a natural, authentic way glorifies God and allows others to see His work in our lives. When it seems like every door has been closed, your faith can act as a powerful tool in your tool kit to drive decisions and actions on your behalf. That which seems impossible becomes possible through faith. The workplace grind can get difficult and frightening at times, but we can count on our strength that comes directly from our faith in God. When we put our faith into action, expect results. Let your faith serve as an inspiration for others of what He is able to do for them.

SELF-LOVE & WELLNESS

Work/life balance is important to your well being. Some of us are so committed to our jobs and titles that it becomes who we are, not just what we do. We are unable to separate the two, working all day and night. Women who flourish in the workplace seem to glow with radiance because they take care of themselves. They understand the importance of self-love. They show up to work ready to rock the day. They get paid and go home. Their inner and outer beauty is aligned appropriately. While they enjoy looking good, prioritizing their health is equally important. Routine health checkups, dental cleanings, a well rounded diet, exercise and rest are pillars for their high quality of life. These women balance their short-term goals with their long-term visions to thrive. They sow good seeds and transform their difficult experiences into gifts to uplift other women in the workplace. Likewise they will not deprive themselves from the joy of connecting with themselves and engaging in activities that nourish their souls.

CHAMPION OTHER WOMEN

When you support other women, magic happens. Empowered women, empower women. The power of a true healthy work relationship requires transparency and authenticity. Women who thrive in the workplace learn to get a handle on their ego and operate with humility. They listen with curiosity and without judgment. They are comfortable being uncomfortable. Successful women foster "give get" relationships and are not afraid to fact check when necessary. Give women the advice they need to hear rather than what they want to hear. Cheer on the other women who strut into the room. Don't waste your time worrying about what others think about you, as you can't please everyone. The bottom line is everyone in the workplace is not going to be your friend. Surround yourself with women who see the best in you. Refrain from fighting a fight you will always lose, as it is not your fight to fight. Take care of yourself. Remember to fill your own cup while making space for others to pour greatness into you!

Silence Is Power

*"A tablebearer revealeth secrets: but he that is of
a faithful spirit concealeth the matter."*
(Proverbs 11:13)

*"You have to learn to get up from the table
when love is no longer being served."*
~ Nina Simone

After three months of working on a very important project,
I decided to share some elements of it with a trusted co-
worker. We already had several interactions where we shared
information and leaned on each other for support. Plus, since
some of our workloads crossed, we had daily huddles scheduled
to review any hot topics. We also exchanged emails throughout
the course of the day, enjoyed lunch together, and shared great
times outside of work. Without a doubt, I believed that our work
partnership was solid.

One day something was different. She was different. There was
no huddle and none of the usual interactions we typically had
prior to our standing meeting with leadership. Instead, she sat
across the conference room table, avoiding eye contact with me.
It was clear something was off, but I didn't think much of it at
that time.

The next thing I knew, this co-worker was presenting the project I had shared with her in confidence to the senior leadership team—she had stolen it right from under me. I was devastated. As I watched her present the project I had spent months building from the ground up, I was frozen. All I could do was sit and wait for the tragedy to end. When she finished, there were a few questions from leadership, mainly about data collection, but when they asked her about budget analysis, it was her turn to freeze because she couldn't answer. I could see the panic on her face. When she had the nerve to look at me to chime in, I was furious.

I began praying, *God's strength is made perfect in weakness* over and over again in my head. I pulled up *my* presentation and began answering the questions that had left her speechless. The leaders, happy with my responses, asked if we had worked together on this project. I had to pull out every ounce of emotional intelligence I had in me. I replied, "Absolutely not!" and went on to tell them that I had shared bits of my research with her some time ago, and she had taken it upon herself to present elements of the project without my consent.

It was time for everyone else in the room to freeze. After the meeting, I approached her and looked her straight in the eye for what felt like five minutes. No words, just a piercing stare. After stumbling over her own words, the only thing she could say was, "I am so sorry."

Later that day, leadership asked me to present the topic and, as they say, the rest is history!

LET YOUR SILENCE BE YOUR SUPERPOWER

When you have a passion project or vision, either personal or professional, choose who you share it with wisely. Your idea is not safe with everyone. You have the strategic advantage and power over information that others do not have, especially when it pertains to you or your work. Not letting others be privy to your idea creates room for mystery and ignites imagination, which is a great thing! Silence is golden and often the better choice.

Silence can serve as a powerful tool in your toolkit. It allows space for you to hear your own thoughts and give ear to God. It unlocks your creativity and brings forth innovative ideas to bloom without distraction. Let your actions speak louder than your words. Unspoken words can be more valuable and effective. When we share our ideas, we share more than words; we share a piece of ourselves. Be patient, you will know the right time to share and the right person to confide in. Listen to your intuition and let it be your guide.

The Gift Of Discernment

"Beware of false prophets, which come to you in
sheep's clothing, but inwardly they are ravening
wolves. Ye shall know them by their fruits."
(Matthew 7:15)

"You've just got to follow your own path. You have to trust
your heart and you have to listen to the warnings."
~ Chaka Khan

Activate your free gift of discernment! It is important to pray and ask God for guidance and understanding–to pay attention to what's going on with our hearts and process our feelings. When we listen to God's direction and guidance, it helps us identify what is best for *our* lives. With so much deception all around us these days, it's more important than ever to consider and discern other people's motives and intentions.

Discernment is God's gift of ability that helps us judge what is vital in the various aspects of our lives such as in the workplace, on a first date, or when making important decisions. It's easy to form conclusions about someone by the way they appear to be, but how do we know if this person, who looks good and smells good, is someone we should form a relationship with? Discernment. That's how.

God expects us to use reason, common sense and trust our intuition. We need to pray about what we want and wait on God's answer. Meanwhile, be observant. Listen and learn. Watch and wait. Your answer will be revealed and God will expose their true character eventually.

Deception is real. I love plums and often buy the plumpest, dark purple, beautiful semi-soft fruit I can find. I enjoy the texture of the mouthfeel and the burst of juicy flavors. I want my plums to not only look good, but to taste good too. I am highly disappointed when I find a perfect-looking plum and bite into it only to experience the exact opposite—bitter, dried up fruit. It's the same with people. Some people tend to be very polished on the outside and draw us in with their appearance, yet we soon learn they are nothing but dried up bitterness and selfishness on the inside.

When we bear good fruit from the inside out there is no doubt it will taste as good as it looks. Discernment helps us find the perfect fruit for us. It is important to pray and ask God for guidance and understanding. To pay attention to what's going on with our hearts and process our feelings.

Put a stop to second guessing yourself and getting caught up with reasoning or justification for the imperfect fruit. Don't let those quick talkers rush you into something crazy, ignoring the red flags to try and discover the good in someone will cost you later. Thoughts we can't reconcile in our minds, we discern with our spirit. When you know, you know.

Overcoming Strongholds Through The Fruit Of The Spirit

"(For the weapons of our warfare are not carnal, but mighty
through God to the pulling down of strong holds.)"
(2 Corinthians 10:4)

"I am not a quitter. I will fight until I drop. It's just a matter
of having some faith in the fact that as long as you are able
to draw breath in the universe, you have a chance."
~ Cicely Tyson

One of the main functions of fruit is to spread seeds to help the plant reproduce. When we look at the fruit of the Spirit from a biblical standpoint, we understand the seeds to be **love, joy, peace, long suffering, gentleness, goodness, faith, meekness,** and **temperance.** Through our relationship with God flows the fruit of the Spirit which produces stronger character, endurance, and grace within us.

On the other hand, a stronghold refers to a mental or emotional state that someone finds difficult to escape or let go. The battle to overcome emotional strongholds is a process that takes time, maybe even years. Life has a way of shutting us down at times. Emotions make us human, embracing them makes us stronger and more resilient. It is important to feel all the feelings, good and bad.

Nothing makes us feel more powerless than when we face an emotional stronghold. Its energy and weight can generate large disturbances in our minds and hearts. An emotional stronghold can come in the form of abandonment, envy, sadness, fear, or anger, to name a few. When emotions become strongholds in our lives and dominate over the fruit of the Spirit, they become problems. Think about those moments when you feel stress or anger toward someone. When we choose to experience them with God's peace through the fruit of the Spirit, we learn to live peaceably with one another. Peace requires boundaries. Pay attention to the signs; sometimes the season has run its course and it may be time to move on.

The best kind of fruit is the fruit of the Spirit. Sometimes things get written in our minds that we can't reconcile. We all experience negative feelings and a variety of inner challenges. But we are warriors. We can fight back with the sword of the Spirit: the word of God. We have to battle whoever and whatever is trying to control our emotions head on. **There is nothing too big for God.** Where there is confusion, we desperately need to walk in the Spirit and count on God's grace and mercy to overcome our emotional strongholds. Good and mature fruit cannot grow from a dead root. We bear good fruit when we allow the word of God to manifest in our spirit.

Don't let the sneaky whispers of strongholds control your mind. Find perspective outside of yourself. Zoom out, but don't zone out! God is your provider, He is always in the midst of your darkness. Open the door when God knocks on your heart and give Him an enthusiastic "Yes!"

Here are some ways the fruit of the Spirit shows up in my life:

★ *Love* is God's presence within me.
★ *Joy* shows up as praise and a cheerful, positive outlook.
★ *Peace* comes from the calmness and contentment living peaceably with others.
★ *Long suffering* is my ability to stay in my body while waiting.
★ *Gentleness* is when I show care for others when I speak and act.
★ *Goodness* is an expression of kindness and generosity toward myself and others.
★ *Faith* is confidence in what I hope for, but have yet to see.
★ *Meekness* is having a humble and selfless attitude.
★ *Tolerance* is when I extend forgiveness and grace to others, finding common ground.

Stay Clothed In The Full Armor Of God

"Wherefore take unto you the whole armour of God, that you may be able to withstand in the evil day, and having done all, to stand. Stand therefore, having your loins girt about with truth and having on the breastplate of righteousness; And your feet shod with the preparation of the gospel of peace; Above all, taking the shield of faith, wherewith ye shall be able to quench all the fiery darts of the wicked. And take the helmet of salvation, and the sword of the Spirit, which is the word of God."
(Ephesians 6:13-17)

"I think that I am a walking testimony that you can have scars. You can go through turbulent times and still have victory in your life."
~ Natalie Cole

The world we live in is full of challenges. We are confronted with environmental, social, political, and economic issues that impact our lives. The expectations of society and the terrifying occurrences happening in the world serve as powerful reminders of the importance of embracing the power and peace of God's protection.

The armor of God is a metaphor for spiritual protection from temptation, spiritual challenges and the struggles of life. It represents the defense we must take in our spiritual lives. The most beautiful armor you can wear is the confidence of knowing you are protected. Therefore, we must fortify ourselves with the protection of God's armor. Each piece represents something mighty and powerful. Through prayer you are maintaining your armor of protection, as well as asking God to place your armor on you everyday. God has poured a source of strength in you. **Receive It. Own It. Wear It Daily!** Be strong in the Lord and the power of His might!

My Black 6.2

*"No weapon that is formed against thee shall
prosper; and every tongue that shall rise against
thee in judgment thou shalt condemn."*
(Isaiah 54:17)

*"You are your first and most important love. If you can't
love and accept yourself, then no one else will be able to."*
~ Angie Stone

When you know you have God's favor, you have unlimited possibilities. Throughout my sixty-two years of life I have learned many valuable lessons. What I love most about life is that I can learn something new everyday and I am not going to be right about everything. I have learned through prayer and emotional intelligence to understand and manage my emotions in an effort to self-motivate and create harmony within myself and others. On my journey, I have experienced micro and macro aggressions, attempts to keep me down, make me small, or change who I am. With God's strength and my faith, I was able to stand tall. I am sharing these strands of stories to inspire you to play at a new level–lighting a spark of hope for you to unlock your faith, and own your potential and your path forward.

When I step out, I announce myself without saying a word. My strut is fierce! Don't get me wrong, my life has had its fair share of ups and downs, but I have always regarded myself as a confident, no nonsense chick. When the circumstances and trials of my life created wimpy insecurities, sorrow and doubt, I held onto my faith. I was reminded through scripture, *"The Lord is my light and my salvation; whom shall I fear?"* (Psalm 27:1)

With my connection to God, I was able to pick myself up and continue strutting on my journey with relentless courage and meaning.

My goal has always been to represent myself with grace. I present myself professionally with a sassy, eccentric edge. My glam pops with colorful, dazzling accessories that turn heads–often clutching my "go girl" pearls as a symbol of wisdom. My strands change depending on my mood and seasons, ranging from wild curly to one-sided fierce buzz cut to adorned #1B single length braids or twists. I know my hair has often been perceived as a part of my racial and ethnic identity, which is a great thing to me. I am confident in the skin I was born in. I know I am capable of the same opportunities as those who don't look like me. I do my best to give other women their flowers. That's how I show up as an authentic, intelligent, educated Black woman. Sometimes you have to show up and show out even when your tires get kicked.

Here are some of the lessons learned behind my story.

WHEN DID YOUR PLANE LAND FROM AFRICA?

The Moment: Culture Shock. From majority to minority just like that! The range of differences was astounding. Caught completely off guard with no one to defend us. A heartbreaking sixth grade year–the year Dad and Mom made the decision to relocate us from Oakland to Newark, California. The year my young life was turned upside down.

<u>Wisdom/Power Tool:</u> My sister and I were greeted with a welcome that was out of this world. We felt so defeated and surrounded by what felt like an entire school of white kids. The questions came from every direction.

"How often do you go to Africa?"
"Do you eat chitlins everyday?"
"Does your skin color change throughout the night?"
"Is your hair made of wool?"
"Are your parents slaves?"

And the ridiculous list goes on and on. We were culture shocked, abandoned, and didn't know how to react. Thank the Lord–we were literally saved by the bell. And it was the same treatment day after day.

We experienced many feelings of anxiety, stress, sadness, frustration and loneliness. It was so bad! We thought our parents hated us. Why would they put us in this situation? We threatened to run away on many occasions. We missed our friends and teachers who looked like us. We cried for weeks–every night, all night.

Things started to shift though as my dad encouraged us to stand up, be confident and fight. He listened and infused us with the power to get up each morning. He gave us the courage to fight. With every question Dad would have an answer to combat the ignorance; understanding there was a severe lack of knowledge among the white students. He told us it was our time to start asking the questions and educating them on who we actually were. We went to school armed and ready to slay the day. It was on. We started asking the questions.

"Does your mom color your eyes every night?"
"Is your skin painted white?"
"Did your mom draw on the freckles on your face?"

Meanwhile unbeknownst to us, our mom and dad were meeting behind the scenes with the principal and school staff to discuss the issue. They presented their concerns as a shared concern. Now that we were more comfortable, Dad guided us to seek understanding–it was time to transfer these experiences into power. We began to have meaningful conversations where we asked questions and learned about the range of human differences including race and ethnicity. This was my introduction to diversity and where I began to learn the variety of differences among people. These pivotal moments and experiences that slipped through the guard rails taught me the awareness of race and what racism is.

I am so proud of my mom and dad. They were very active and involved in our life and cared about us and the community at large. They made their voices heard. They stayed very active in church and forged great friendships. They continued to raise awareness through service, purpose and commitment. They were a part of a grassroot effort to bring social justice to the area and Dad later became the first president of the NAACP for the tri-city area, which included Newark, Fremont, and Union City.

My dad is eighty-nine years old today. When reflecting on his acts of service throughout the years, he says his greatest accomplishments were building community, breaking through some of the educational barriers at schools, and holding employers accountable for hiring Blacks in their communities. He brought Black and white people of the community together to collaborate on views of racial discrimination and barriers to Black progress. He sat at the table and got things done. He fought a good fight to advance policies and practices that expanded human rights. Growing up in Georgia, my mom and dad were quite familiar with being deprived of access to privileges and opportunity. Dad was, and still is, very proud of his accomplishments.

The older I get the more I appreciate how I was raised and who raised me. Together, Mom and Dad loved us unconditionally. They laid a great foundation even though times were rough–sacrificing and struggling to raise a family of six–they made sure we never felt it. And, through it all, they always pushed us to do more, while believing that we could.

NEW TITLE, NO MONEY

The Moment: "Congratulations we would like to promote you! Um, but you won't see a salary increase for six months." Being promoted without financial compensation because they wanted me to "prove myself" is known as a "dry promotion." And it is an exercise my white colleagues weren't asked to complete.

Wisdom/Power Tool: My Power. My Choice! I had to remove the emotion and consider my alternatives. First and foremost, I had to stand up and have my voice heard by sharing my disappointment and asking about the why–forcing them to put the bias into words. My next step was to decide whether to accept, negotiate or decline the offer. Consideration: a promotion with new responsibilities, demands and expectations, and without *any* financial incentives.

While I enjoyed the job, I knew taking this promotion without a pay increase would leave me feeling underappreciated, undervalued and resentful. The answer was no. I declined the promotion, resigned, retained my power and searched for a company that would give me what I was worth.

YOU CAN'T BE YOU HERE

The Moment: Tone it down! Code switching– changing who I was to be accepted by others who didn't look like me and avoid being perceived as the "angry Black woman." Avoid my passion being translated as anger.

Wisdom/Power Tool: Your enthusiasm sometimes gets in the way of your work. At the same time you're asked to bring your "happy" to work. *How contradicting is that?* Think before you speak! They would say it was my body language and tone. I talk with my hands and can be very animated in my delivery, a quality that often resulted in being perceived as an upset and unhappy Black woman. It didn't have anything to do with my happiness.

Being the only Black woman in the room, I found myself downplaying or toning down certain aspects of my personality to put others at ease. Sometimes I would have a little "code switch moment" depending on the dominant audience. It became very exhausting and frustrating to think about how to respond in a way that did not make me be perceived as an angry Black woman. As a manager it got to a point where I would stay quiet in meetings, yet always prepared to provide input when necessary.

During that time, I found it important to transfer my experience to those few frontline workers who looked like me. I took the liberty to train them up. I coached them on everything from dress code to business etiquette to acceptable language, and, of course, how to bring their "happy" to work!

BLACK HANDS/ BLURRED FACE

<u>The Moment</u>: When it came to lifestyle photography, my Black hands and blurred out Black face became the most important thing in the photoshoot. The unspoken expectation of representing the entire Black race was clear: I was a tool rather than a person. I was them "doing better." But no one will ever have the opportunity to shrink me that way. I held them accountable to seeing me as a person rather than a tool. Even so, I was definitely outnumbered and needing others who looked like me.

<u>Wisdom/Power Tool</u>: Love the skin you're in. As the saying goes "what you see is what you get." The lack of diversity in an organization's stock images and social media channels isn't just an image problem, it's a cultural problem. Without them it's hard for you to believe you are important to the company. Yet my Black face was often called to step up to the podium to help defend or check the box for the company's "so called" DEI program.

There was only heightened awareness around their biases when guests—other people of color—complained about mistreatment during visits. Only then did my Black voice and Black skin become relevant as they urged me to help them de-escalate the issue.

Listen and learn. Sometimes you have to manage up. This is where I used my voice, having a heart to serve, I became a soundboard to the external customers who looked like me to bring these areas of concern to the internal leadership team. Small change, but at the very least it set a framework for transparency.

TURNING HEADS

<u>The Moment</u>: When drama comes from women of color. "Who does she think she is?" The question I always ask in response is

"Who are *you*?" I am not going to apologize for who I am. I refuse to tolerate your passive aggressive behavior. This has nothing to do with me, and has everything to do with you. Deal with your jealousy, bitterness, and envy on your own!

Wisdom/Power Tool: Don't automatically assume that all Black people will bend over backwards to support or even speak to you just because you are Black. Protecting myself from destructive energy and staying in my lane is who I am. For me, it is more hurtful when drama comes from women of color, particularly those who attempt to rally support from others.

To be crystal clear, how can we expect others to respect us when we are not willing to support or give our people their flowers and celebrate them. Stop hating. Stop trying to one up them. When your Sistas walk in the room, give them their "go girl" moment, pull them up rather than tear them down. They are counting on you to stand by them. Sadly, not every connection will be life-changing in a positive way. Sometimes you won't feel connected regardless of color. Think about the broad shoulders you stood on to get where you are, and remember we are stronger together!

WHEN MY LAST NAME CHANGED FROM TERRY TO YOUNG

The Moment: Showing up for the job interview. "Excuse me, what did you say your last name was again?" (Hmm… her face doesn't look like her last name.)

Wisdom/Power Tool: People often think your name gives clues to the color of your face. Stereotypes in society can lead people to falsely believe certain names belong to certain faces. There was a lot of confusion when I showed up to interview for a position, the look of surprise or even disgust was painfully obvious. While I went through the interview, it was evident I didn't have "the look" they wanted. Even though my experience met the qualifications for the job, the rejection letter was in the mail before I made it home.

Hiring should focus on a candidate's skills and have a lens toward developing diversity in the existing culture. The origin of your name doesn't necessarily determine your ethnicity. Not only do surnames not reveal the identity of your ancestors, they do not provide the details of your life. This is not for an employer to judge!

I had lots of fun with this bias. When I would make dinner reservations for my team under my name, the restaurant often thought I was Sheila Young, the acting mayor of San Leandro at the time. In anticipation of their esteemed guest, they would roll out the red carpet and have all of the frills in place. The fun came when I arrived and it was clear I wasn't the Sheila Young they were expecting. While some places would continue the "wow moments" after learning I wasn't the mayor, others acted as if I had committed a crime. Knowing that I wasn't to blame for the mix-up, I had fun collecting lots of selfies and funny stories along the way.

"CAN I FEEL OR TOUCH YOUR HAIR?"

<u>The Moment</u>: Inappropriate touching, assumed ownership, lack of personal space, being treated like a pet instead of a person. All microaggressions at play. You touched it once, but you do not get the right to pet the Black girl's hair every time she changes her hairstyle. Touching a Black person's hair without permission, promotes the idea that we are free to be treated differently.

<u>Wisdom/Power Tool</u>: Hands off. Respect the hair game please! I'm not yours to touch. I own my mind, body and spirit–not you! I had many of these unprofessional moments–running across many white girls and coworkers who would often ask to touch my hair every time I changed my hair style. When I asked why, they would reply, "I am curious. I just want to see what it feels like." And you know you always get that one who says, "My one Black friend..."

That part. It made me feel as if they were feeding into the tale that white hair is normal and anything else is abnormal. When I said no to their ridiculous request, they would look at me as if I was the one with the problem.

I will never forget the day when I flipped the script on them. On this particular day, I was rocking short twists. I began to educate them by explaining that my Black hair is not made of wool, but it's textured and it is versatile, which allows me to create various unique styles. I must say they were stunned with my response, but also curious and trying to gain understanding. OMG, I'm not exaggerating when I say it became a "Black hair in-service moment". My goal was to drive home the point that my hair is a symbol of my identity and creative expression–a truly teachable moment that needed to be had. In all due respect, I empowered them to go spread the word to their white friends and family that it is disrespectful and unprofessional to touch or ask to touch anyone's Black hair!

PART TWO

*"He giveth power to the faint; and to them that
have no might he increaseth strength."
(Isaiah 40:29)*

PART TWO

Forgiveness Is For You

"Let all bitterness, and wrath, and anger, and clamour,
and evil speaking, be put away from you, with all malice,
and be kind one to another tenderhearted, forgiving one
another, even as God for Christ's sake has forgiven you."
(Ephesians 4:31-32)

"Let's shake free this gravity of judgment, and
fly high on the wings of forgiveness."
~ India Arie Simpson

Over the years I've forgiven myself and many others, but how do you forgive someone who robbed you at knifepoint?

I will never forget that day. I was on my way to Southern California and had pulled over to make a quick call when an old, white Chevrolet Chevette appeared out of nowhere. Before I knew it, the tip of a knife was pressed up against my stomach, a loud roaring voice demanded money, and a hand snatched the jewelry off my arm and neck. Then he grabbed my purse, jumped back into the Chevette and drove off to his next victim. A two-minute experience felt like an hour. I was trembling with fear, confusion, and anger.

Before driving home, I filed a police report. About an hour after arriving home, a police officer called. He said they had arrested the scumbag who robbed me. Apparently, he had robbed a few others and assaulted a jogger. I remember lifting my hands and thanking the Lord. I was glad they caught him and ready to be done with it all.

A few days later, I received a certified subpoena to testify and an airline ticket to fly back to Southern California. Good Lord, what a scary experience it is to have the man who robbed you rocking back and forth in his chair, staring at you with demonic yellow-green eyes. I was shaking in my boots! The DA was confident the defendant would be locked up for years because of his long history of robbery and attempted murder charges. Instead, he was sentenced to three months. I couldn't believe it.

I felt every emotion you can imagine feeling. Anxiety, paranoia and insomnia from PTSD were my constant companions. It was difficult to find strength after this ordeal, the thought of him having my wallet and identification with my address was beyond scary. I leaned on my family and pastor for emotional support. When my pastor spoke to me about forgiveness, I could not fathom the idea. Instead my neck snapped with a serious eye roll as I thought to myself, *Pastor must be kidding me.*

What happened shook me to my core. It was difficult to understand that forgiving the robber would free me from the negative emotions I was feeling. While my family's support was awesome and helped a lot, I had to dig deep to find my own strength. When I finally chose to forgive, it created a space to heal from the anxiety and stress. This process helped me learn that forgiveness isn't about the other person, it's about healing my own heart.

● WHY IS FORGIVENESS FOR *YOU*?

We all want to feel loved and appreciated. When someone offends, hurts or harms us, it's human nature to want to get back at them. Oftentimes we can fall into a pattern of toxic unforgiveness, harboring resentment and bitterness in our hearts, spending countless hours plotting out a plan to get the person back, or waiting for them to fail or suffer. It is the vicious thoughts of pain, wounds, hurt, betrayal, disgust, and anger that replay in our minds, which I call emotional strongholds, that hinder us from letting go. We hold onto a grudge and cling to those thoughts and feelings that harm us, while the other person has moved on. Even when we try to forgive it can be difficult for us to do so, especially when we've invested so much time and energy into our emotional strongholds. This is where prayer is essential, as on our own we are tempted to wander back to unforgiveness.

While forgiveness can be complicated and challenging, it is the sweetest form of revenge. When you forgive, you give up all rights to getting even with the person who hurt you. Praying for the person who hurts you sounds crazy, yet it is a necessary step in the process of letting go and choosing to move forward. We know we can depend on God's grace and mercy to dissolve all negative emotions and to forgive the person who hurt or offended us. I believe this is where true transformation takes place.

CHOOSE TO LET GO WITH ZERO EXPECTATIONS

Forgiveness is necessary to create closure and reclaim *our* power. The act of forgiving is critical to our emotional wellbeing. It frees us from bondage and removes us from feelings of anger and resentment. Forgiveness allows us to leave what belongs in the past, in the past. It allows us to focus on our present and future with peace of mind. Forgiveness ultimately sets us free!

"Do not be overcome by evil, but overcome evil with good."
(Romans 12:21)

Woosah Moments

"...Come ye yourselves apart into a
desert place, and rest a while."
(Mark 6:31)

"It's important that you love and respect yourself first."
~ *Gladys Knight*

A *Woosah Moment* is precious time set aside just for me to get back in my body, replenish my cup, and fix my own crown. A *Woosah Moment* can take place indoors or outdoors, and range from a few minutes to several hours or days. It is a true form of "Relax-Relate-Release!" This is where being selfish is a good and powerful thing–self-care at its best. A small task resulting in a feeling of calm and peace.

Here are just a few of the *Woosah Moments* I use to make the rollercoaster of life, which never seems to slow down, come to a screeching halt.

RESET AND REJUVENATE (RELAX)

A warm bubble bath gives me a sense of calm and comfort. Sometimes I take my bath time up a notch by creating a mood such as, "Let it go, *girl*," and preparing my mind in advance. I enjoy being creative with this time–enhancing the atmosphere, lighting softly-scented candles, playing calm music and using fluffy spa towels. I stay hydrated with a tall glass of cold water infused with lemon slices. I am never stingy with the bubbles in the water–the more, the better. Sometimes I toss in a handful of rose petals, adding another level of ambiance. Keeping with the theme of "Let it go, *girl*," my bath time may include spending a few minutes journaling (while in the tub), meditation, turning on the jets, putting on a face mask, and adjusting my bath pillow to enjoy an awesome soak. Soon I am off to la-la land where my mind remains at peace. Afterwards I let the stress float down the drain while I wrap myself in a fluffy towel.

SOOTHING, FRESH AND SALTY (RELATE)

I get a thrill driving along the winding roads of the California coast. I love relaxing on the beach and smelling the fresh salty ocean. I love sliding my feet through the grainy sand, watching the curls of the waves, and listening to their rippling roars. I love being motionless, kicking back, enjoying the beauty of God's curtains made up of white fluffy marshmallow clouds in the sky above. I appreciate the light of the ocean and the beauty of its fullness. I release my thoughts from my heart through prayer and let every request be known to God. Oftentimes I get acknowledgement from God that he heard my prayers and his hand is at work from the sun that peeks out from the clouds.

THE LOST ART OF HANDWRITTEN
LOVE LETTERS (RELEASE)

Nowadays we are so preoccupied with our smartphones and computers, we are losing the art of handwritten notes and letters. Sending handwritten cards and love notes to my family and friends is a big thing for me. There is something special about a handwritten letter for both the sender and receiver. For me, it is therapeutic and meditative when I offload my thoughts on paper hoping to bring a smile or change the course of someone's day. In addition to sending handwritten letters, I have enjoyed being sneaky and creative over the years by leaving a funny handwritten note in my daughter's lunch box, writing a sexy love note to my honey on the mirror with red lipstick, and placing a colorful note of appreciation on my coworkers' desks or in the breakroom. The excitement of receiving and reading a handwritten letter is special and will be remembered long after it is tossed in the trash or erased from the mirror.

She's Showered In Power

"A friend loveth at all times,..."
(Proverbs 17:17)

"Everyone has a gift for something, even if it
is the gift of being a good friend."
~ Marian Anderson

G rowing up, my dad would often tell us, "Consider yourself lucky if you find at least one friend in a lifetime."

We get our family by chance and our friends by choice. My first best friend was my sister. From the beginning, our bond was strong. We brought out the best in each other. Being eleven months apart, we would often call ourselves twins, yet we had our own identities and were blessed to have a separate circle of friends. She and I were always there for each other through thick and thin. Together we took the world by storm. We were very adventurous and had a mutual love for fashion (and our trend setting, out-of-the-box fashion game is still on fleek to this day).

Throughout our school ages, my sister was heavily involved in the arts, theater, and sports, while cheerleading, sports, and student government were my thing. Our parents had instilled in us the importance of serving beyond ourselves at a very young age. We certainly took full advantage to serve and have fun. We made it a priority to break bread together, enjoying a lovely breakfast every Saturday morning. Our weekends were spent hosting girls workshops or preparing for neighborhood talent shows and church plays. Our favorite pastimes were grilling on the beach, traveling, enjoying concerts at the Circle Star and Berkeley Greek Theaters, or having funk attacks watching the mothership land at George Clinton's P-Funk concerts at the Oakland Coliseum. We were, and still are, the life of any party.

My brothers were my best friends too, and I loved my relationship with them—it was and still is comedy central whenever we chat by phone or are in each other's company. My brothers were always my biggest fans and in my corner, yet quick to check me when needed. They were special comrades in my life and my voice of reason particularly when it came to policing my outfits. Ready to report to mom if they thought my dress was too short or my blouse revealed too much. They were very protective and did their best to shield me from any hurt or harm.

My older brother was an artist and highly imaginative. I enjoyed weekend getaways with friends at his eclectic and cozy apartments. He was our guaranteed ride to the popular Phase 3 Kid Disco and took the blame for missed curfews. I must say, it was sometimes difficult to have my younger brother tag along as his humor and sarcastic jokes were funny, but often annoying and piercing to others—that part! But when it came to spinning and scratching on two turntables and a microphone, my younger brother nailed it. He was the best DJ ever. He brought energy to all of our house parties and those rap battles were epic—he brung home the trophy every time. He also loved sports, particularly baseball, and he was great at it. We would often come home with a hoarse voice after screaming with excitement because of all his home runs!

FRIENDSHIPS COME IN ALL SHAPES, COLORS AND SIZES

Meeting people and striking up a conversation comes naturally for me. I am known to be very social, coupled with a big personality and a high level of positive energy. Through trial and error, I have learned I can't force a friendship nor can a friendship be forced upon me. Everyone you meet will not qualify as a friend. I have met so many people throughout my life and have a variety of friends. Childhood friends, fun friends, tedious friends, soul sistas, lifelong friends, seasonal friends, work friends, school friends, and, of course, the best friend and the best friend forever-your ride and live friends. Many are still in my life to this day. Regardless of the type of friend, these are people I value and share a special bond.

A FRIENDSHIP BREAKUP CAN MAKE YOU FEEL WOBBLY AND OFF-BALANCED

Throughout our lives, friends will come and go. They can be around for a reason, a season, or a lifetime. What you thought would be a friendship that would last forever may change. That was my story with one friend. A best friend forever. An amazing blessing in my life who made my smile brighter, my laugh louder, and my life better. Until one day when it came to an abrupt end after almost thirty years. While there were some signs things were changing—a sudden move, shifting priorities, and lots of false accusations that did not quite add up—I was still surprised when our friendship eventually fizzled away.

It's still a mystery that I will never fully understand. Sadly, I may never know the reason why our friendship ended. As painful as it was, I allowed myself to feel all of the feelings, gave myself time to heal, and refused to be a revolving door to the unhealthy burdens, as they were not my load to carry. In the end, I am very grateful for the time we shared, thanking God for the cherished memories that will keep my heart smiling and laughing for the rest of my life!

TRUE FRIENDSHIP: A JOURNEY WITHOUT AN END!

She is showered in power! Girlfriends, what would we do without them? They are rare finds. Everyone needs a Soul Sista, a connected spirit who offers love and acceptance. She sees you and needs you. She reminds you of your beauty when you can't see it yourself. She shows up as her authentic self. She supports you with love, not just words.

She pushes you to do difficult, complicated things. She lets her guard down in the midst of a storm and trusts she is safe. She has a panoramic view of your life and runs interference genuinely with intention when needed. She runs offense in the friendship instead of defense. When you are in your quiet, she understands and doesn't make it about her. She fills your cup with grace and allows you to reciprocate. She turns your frown into a smile and her soul says yes! She guarantees that every text message will be hit with encouraging words such as:

"Hello beautiful, I'm here for you."
"Yes, Queen, you've got this."
"Look at God, twist and twirl girl."
"Go on with your bad self."
"You are amazing, the world is better because you're in it."

Together in laughter, united in love. She gives you the flowers you deserve!

Less Of Them, More Of Me

"Comfort your hearts, and stablish you in
every good word and work."
(2 Thessalonians 2:17)

"If you are unhappy with anything... Whatever is bringing
you down, get rid of it. Because you'll find that when you're
free, your true creativity, your true self, comes out."
~ Tina Turner

Letting go of a toxic relationship can be challenging, but it is a vital step toward maintaining your power. Stand your ground! Toxic people love to gaslight you and will do whatever it takes to be the hero/victim, even if their actions or words hurt you. It becomes obvious real quick you are not a priority. You are constantly giving with no love or respect in return. They only come around when they're in need. You don't connect on the same level. What's the point?

COMPROMISE SHOULDN'T COME AT THE COST OF YOUR HAPPINESS

Being flexible is one thing, but if someone jeopardizes your overall well-being they are not healthy to be around. You deserve to be whole and happy; don't settle for less. Protect your time and energy from toxicity. Relationships, including those with family members, work best when there is commonality and mutual interests. It's important to surround yourself with thinkers and doers who see you and the greatness ahead of you.

No matter how uncomfortable it might be, find ways to put yourself first. It is absolutely okay to be selfish when it comes to protecting your time and energy. Don't feel guilty about putting yourself first, after all the number one safety rule on every flight is to put your mask on first before assisting others. The decision is ultimately in your hands. Don't take on responsibility for others' failings.

As a general rule, don't let everyone's business become your business because it's not yours to carry. Lean into the attitude of *less of them, more of me*. Stay prayed up!

Don't Be A Bystander In Your Own Life

"...The harvest truly is plenteous, but the labourers are few;"
(Matthew 9:37)

"Always remember you have within you the
strength, the patience and the passion to
reach for the stars to change the world."
~ Harriet Tubman

Turn the camera towards yourself because you are the star of your life! You are the most important person in your life. You are too amazing to be the only thing standing in your way! Life is a journey filled with unlimited opportunities, challenges and decisions. The good news is that God has already created you, so you don't need to recreate what He has already made. Isn't it time to get off the sideline—watching things happen to you and all around you—without doing anything to help yourself?

EXECUTE YOUR POWER

Every journey begins with a step, so get to stepping! Start putting yourself first and stop neglecting your own needs. There is no need to be afraid of yourself and your capabilities. You have the power to shape your destiny and make choices. Invest in yourself. Consider going back to school, taking a class, starting a business, or networking with others in your field of interest. It's never too late to be what you want to be. Make a plan and stick to it. If we don't make a plan and diligently work on that plan, it won't happen. Instead of blaming other people, the economy, or the government for your circumstances, take time to understand that you have control over your life situations, which gives you the power to change them. Isn't that awesome?

FIND YOUR SWEET SPOT

Hone in on what you enjoy and value. Think of things where your ambition, passion and strength will lead you to gratification and financial security. When you choose your own path you learn about consequences. There will be growth throughout the process. Stay in tune with yourself and work for it. It may not be easy, and you may have to change course a few times, but that's certainly okay.

YOU DON'T NEED A TROPHY TO HAVE PRIDE IN YOURSELF

Rather than being a bystander in your life, get up, turn the knob, open the door, step in, and take control of your life. Whatever you choose to do, do it with the enthusiasm of an excited child. Know that God will break every curse that prevents you from moving forward. It's time to let others know that you are going places. Let your courage and drive serve as a catalyst to motivate and inspire others. It is yours for the making. Keep the faith, and believe it can be done.

Unleash The Strut
From The Inside Out

*"Strength and honor are her clothing and she shall
rejoice in time to come. She openeth her mouth with
wisdom; and in her tongue is the law of kindness."*
(Proverbs 31:25-26)

*"The kind of beauty I want most is the hard-to-get kind
that comes from within: strength, courage, dignity."*
~ Ruby Lee

D are to Dazzle! Style is an extension of my personality and
has been in my DNA since I can remember. I was born on
a cold Connecticut morning in December. My mom says I was
a little sassy fashionista from day one. I even dressed up to go to
the playground. When it was time for me to start kindergarten,
the criteria back then was that you had to be five years old prior
to December 1. I didn't make the cut, but my mom had different
criteria. She felt I was ready for school and was very persistent
trying to get me in.

One day when we were picking up my brother, she approached the
school principal and shared her desire for me to start school the
following year. The principal crouched down and started asking

me a list of questions including my name, address, age, as well as a list of general skills and educational questions. Now, I must share that prior to picking up my brother, my sister and I had been playing dress up and my strut was real at age four. I was all dolled up in a dress, my mom's dangling pearls, her high heeled shoes, and my lips were topped with her red lipstick. Needless to say, my confidence and poise impressed the principal, an agreement was reached, and I was able to start school a year early.

DRESSING FOR SUCCESS MATTERS

Strut in the room like God dispatched you there! Appearance is a form of self-care. When you feel good about yourself it shows in your general demeanor, it draws positive attention, and promotes self-confidence. Presenting your inner beauty on the outside is extremely important. When you present yourself to the world, present the true you, not just with your clothes, but with everything you do. We can put on a Gucci suit and look like a million dollars, but if we don't feel good about ourselves inside it will be reflected on the outside. Does your inner beauty line up with your get up? Inner beauty is expressed in how we treat ourselves and others. It stretches beyond our physical appearance and is reflected through acts of kindness, compassion, and love.

We all have our own unique style; yes, even *you*! We all have the ability to choose looks and clothing based on trends we like, colors we look good in, and what makes us feel fabulous. Ultimately, style is a way to express our true selves. There are numerous styles for you to mix and match and create the professional, classic, vintage, preppy, or fun styles you want to wear. Remember to include the full armor of God. Acknowledge, explore and *Unleash the Strut*!

Here are a few powerful tips to *Unleash the Strut* and showcase your inner and outer beauty.

Outer Beauty:

★ Know your body type (be curious and stay objective).
★ Invest in timeless neutral pieces.
★ Be critical of what you love in your current wardrobe.
★ Own what colors look good on you and how they inspire you.
★ Take some creative risks. Try it on, welcome it to your body, and embrace it.

Inner Beauty:

★ Say something nice to the person in the mirror everyday.
★ Spend time focusing on what makes you feel good about yourself.
★ Show compassion to others.
★ Conduct an "Is this serving me?" audit of your social media habits.
★ Accept people for who they are.

Go on, girl. I see you turning heads when you walk into the room!

Be A Good Steward
Of Your Money

"But my God shall supply all your needs according
to his riches in glory by Christ Jesus."
(Philippians 4:19)

"I don't have to be wealthy to be rich – my
spirit is a valuable commodity."
~ Eartha Kitt

As a style coach, I am always shopping for fabulous styles, but in my early entrepreneur days I found myself derailed from the goal, becoming my own VIP client with a cart filled with two of everything. One for me, one for the client. You name it, I bought it. My little rainy day fund started dwindling fast, which made it difficult for me to achieve my monthly budget.

After much prayer, I started to adjust various areas of my life through financial fasting–a process of improving my spending habits by focusing on need versus want, giving up all unnecessary spending habits. It took me a while to trust and believe the situation would come to pass. The Lord inspired me to find peace and comfort in the things I already had in my closet. More is not always better. Decluttering and rediscovering items helped me create new looks with the clothes I forgot I loved. It also allowed me to enhance the diversity of my wardrobe, saving me time, money, and frustration while leveling up my style game. Now I find myself geeking out on finances, recording every penny spent.

"Take heed, and beware of covetousness: for
a man's life consisteth not in the abundance
of the things which he possesseth."
(Luke 12:15)

The journey towards financial security begins with you. Be a steward of your money. Start living within your means and managing your money with intention. Watch how it is spent, and how it is earned. Yes, it can be a challenging task, but the discipline will allow you to enjoy greater security in your life, today, tomorrow, and for years to come. Set your budget and explore ways to invest wisely. You are never too old or too young to start.

Invest wisely, even if it's a small amount. Anything you can set aside will eventually stack up. Numbers do not lie. Ask yourself *what are the things I spend too much money on?* Be honest and deal with them one at a time.

MONEY, MONEY, MONEY, MONEY, MONEY!

The Ojays describe it best in their hit single, "For The Love Of Money" where they share a valuable lesson to heed: money changes relationships. Lending money to family and friends can be a gesture of goodwill when someone you know is in a tight spot, but it can be complicated if your efforts to assist lead to disagreements or you experience a financial tight spot as a result of lending. I don't lend money anymore. If someone asks to borrow money, and it's a legitimate request, and I have the means to do so, I "gift" what I can to help, rather than loan. In my "yes" I give without any attachments. I've learned not to risk damaging a trusted relationship or losing a friend by putting myself in the awkward situation of repeatedly asking for my money back. I am also clear about my "no." I don't make excuses anymore. "No" is a complete sentence. Excuses and other words are unnecessary. However, I do offer to pray for their situation.

THE BOTTOM LINE

Before lending money to friends and family, consider how it could affect you financially and emotionally. You work hard for your money, if you are going to loan it out, think about the consequences and risks, particularly if they don't pay you back. Loaning money can damage relationships with your friends and family. This emotional trauma will feel worse than losing the money. In the words of The Ojays, "For a small piece of paper, it carries a lot of weight."

Additionally, there are many ways to sow seeds through tithing, time, talents, skills, caring and giving to those less fortunate. Even during tough times, consider sharing your blessings with others. This can bring joy to your life while making a positive impact in the lives of others.

While sowing seeds, remember your health is an investment. Your return on investment will be higher the earlier you invest. Managing your health gives you a chance to enjoy a higher quality, brighter life longer.

PART THREE

"Knowing this, that the trying of
your faith worketh patience."
(James 1:3)

PART THREE

Seasons

"A time to be born, and a time to die; a time to plant, and a time to pluck up which is planted; A time to kill, and a time to heal; a time to break down, and a time to build up; A time to weep, and a time to laugh; a time to mourn, and a time to dance; A time to cast away stones, and a time to gather stones together; a time to embrace, and a time to refrain from embracing; a time to get, and a time to lose, a time to keep, and a time to cast away; A time to rend, and a time to sew; a time to keep silence, and a time to speak; A time to love, and a time to hate; a time of war, and a time of peace."
(Ecclesiastes 3:2-12)

"No matter what comes, I am staying and standing."
~ Bessie Coleman

God wants us to have joy in every season of our life. Seasons help things change whether it's subtle or sporadic, it's change. The changing of seasons is an exciting time for new beginnings. There are differences related to each season that provide us with the opportunity to enjoy the changes in the foods we eat, the activities we do, the styles we wear, and, of course, the weather we experience.

Embracing the seasons internally and externally requires us to slow down and take notice of the beauty changing around us. It's a perfect time to tune ourselves into the energy of each season by spending time aligning our diets, decorating our homes with seasonal essentials, spending time with nature, and enjoying traditional celebrations with family.

In the seasons of life there will be ups and downs, happy and sad times, times that inspire peace, and times that bring pain.

> *"To every thing there is a season, and a time*
> *to every purpose under the heaven."*
> *(Ecclesiastes 3:1)*

We will experience circumstances in life, which are not by accident, but intentionally orchestrated by God with great purpose. These seasons may be difficult to understand. When you go through an easy season, embrace the good and praise God. When you're in a difficult season, embrace what matters most and receive the help God offers. Let Him empower you to endure. It can be a sign God is moving you in a new direction. You may feel like you're in a waiting period, but pray for patience and know that God is about to do something new. Get ready to enjoy a bountiful season ahead!

Literally Working 9-5

"Lo, children are an heritage of the Lord:..."
(Psalm 127:3)

"Women and girls can do whatever they want. There is
no limit to what we as women can accomplish."
~ Michelle Obama

The day my daughter was born was the best day of my life. My water broke at 9:00 a.m. and she took her first breath at 5:00 p.m. She was perfect! I was both excited and serious about my new role as a mother. I knew I had to protect, teach, and support her, as well as be a good moral compass for her, and I was emotionally prepared for the task. I understood being a mom was a privilege, a gift from God. As a mom there is nothing more magical than watching your baby grow and explore their world. My daughter and I were inseparable and she amazed me every day!

Being a mom taught me to be more patient, more loving, and more appreciative of every moment we shared together. Motherhood makes you strong and courageous. It's the kind of inner strength that can only stem from the depth of love, care, and responsibility from being a mom.

A Steep Rocky
Mountain Ahead

"Fear thou not; for I am with thee: be not dismayed; for I am thy God: I will strengthen thee; yea, I will help thee; yea, I will uphold thee with the right hand of my righteousness."
(Isaiah 41:10)

*"Instead of looking at the past, I put myself
ahead twenty years and try to look at what I
need to do now in order to get there then."*
~ Diana Ross

Fast-forward to three years later when I began the divorce process. Patience is the key to any exit plan. I thought leaving would make it better quickly, instead it was the beginning of a living disaster.

With my daughter in tow, I found myself resting on the bottom level of a bunk bed at my sister's house wondering if this nightmare I was living would ever end. My mom had recently relocated to the East Coast on a job transfer. I needed her so much, but my sister and her family welcomed us with open arms, and I had my wise counsel and friends. Collectively, they filled my cup with assurances that "this too would pass." They kept their foot on the pedal and made sure I was steadfast in navigating the journey with faith. They fixed my crown, propped me up, and pushed me to show up each day without option. As a single mom, I was not afraid of parenting. As a methodical, risk-averse person, the unknown road ahead scared the living daylights out of me.

I was broken, trying to resign to my faith. My days were long and full of thoughts. I had many sleepless nights and my mind was all over the place. When I was alone the only thing that seemed to quiet my noisy spirit was a brisk walk through the neighborhood listening to the sounds of the chirping birds, whistling breeze, busy streets, and the constant motion of the swaying trees. I also loved to dance; it brought me joy. Through dance my body could articulate words I couldn't express. Music calmed my thoughts. Partying and drinking became a temporary mood boost, a great mental escape. Once I returned home though, the frustration, sadness, and hurt would reappear in my heart. Don't get me wrong, I knew everyday wasn't going to be a fairy tale, but I was ready to wake up from the nightmare.

I attended church every Sunday, but my faith still waned. Laying in bed, under the blanket in the fetal position, felt like a better escape. However, my role on the Usher Board kept me connected to being of service and to guest experience, both of which were really important to me. I prayed continually for God to order my steps. I continued to show up for work where I had great benefits and a decent salary, which would turn out to be much needed blessings.

A few weeks after I moved into my sister's home, I walked out the front door to learn my car had been repossessed. Two weeks later, a process server came to my job and served me a judgment. And the hits kept coming. Over the next few weeks, three garnishments were taken from my paycheck, checks bounced left and right, and my bank account was eventually frozen. I received many calls from creditors; it was a nasty situation. I felt crazy with emotion and that the tears would never stop falling. I hoped to find wisdom that would make everything right in my brain, but thoughts like *failure* and *loser* overshadowed my mind. Everyday I felt worse. There were days where my once steady voice quivered and I couldn't connect with the words coming out of my mouth. My power button was off. My issue wasn't the separation, it was the mountain in front of me that felt too steep to climb. Co-parenting did not exist, becoming a toxic tug-of-war that carried on for years, impacting my daughter in a multitude of ways. I knew I could have done a better job at communicating and collaborating more effectively, but it takes two. I tried to cope, but I wasn't being the best version of myself and many around me became the targets of my unpleasant, condescending behavior. Bubbly Sheila was shrinking. I was a functioning hot mess. My light was so dim. During this time I learned a lot about friendship—who was down, who was hanging around, and who was hoping to get a piece of my leftovers.

Trying to cope with everyday life was tough and dealing with a bitter divorce was crippling me to my core. We refused to compromise and fought over everything, from the home to the silverware. It was a costly price to pay. I had made the mistake of putting my feelings above the best interests of my daughter. I forgot my number one priority was to protect her. If I could've rewritten my script, my narrative would have been so different. I would have handled things more maturely. Instead, the custody battle for my daughter got real, quick. Our inability to cooperate with each other resulted in a six and six month custody order, meaning I would have custody for half the year, and he would have custody the other half. I went absolutely nuts! While we tried to maintain consistency between the two households, it did not always work. Differing parenting styles made everything confusing and overwhelming for my daughter. We had this arrangement for two years before we were able to reach a more amicable agreement.

Through my prayers, and the prayer warriors who prayed over me, I finally began to refocus my energies from partying like a rockstar back to an attitude of *Stop! Enough! Focus! Prioritize Yourself* and *Handle Your Business!* I developed a better understanding of myself. The reality of my situation became crystal clear and my faith pushed me to trust and believe that this wasn't the end of my story. I made my wants known to God by speaking my desires into existence. I fell to my knees praying for a sound mind and faith over worry. I asked the Lord to keep my daughter and me in His care, and to repair the hole in my heart. I began journaling my thoughts, setting timelines for my comeback, both mentally and financially. Without a doubt, I was sure God was going to bring it all to pass. Once I started being consistent in my walk of faith, I was more open to change. I let myself go when I was journaling. The girl in the mirror started to look familiar again, and the mountain ahead didn't feel too steep to climb.

During this season, I resisted counseling for a long time. I viewed it as a sign of weakness and thought I didn't need someone in a white coat to help me solve my life situations. It was my mom who convinced me that I didn't have to manage myself when there was help available. She assured me it was the right thing to do given the circumstances, so I eventually found myself sitting on the couch seeking help. Speaking with a therapist was incredibly beneficial for my mental wellness. My therapist was a seasoned, brilliant, Christian woman who looked like me. She shared tools that helped me understand my feelings and navigate my emotions courageously. Through many sessions, I was able to acknowledge my own pain and affirm my truth. It enhanced my overall well-being and, more importantly, it gave me the hope and strength I needed to get back into the driver seat. I released the things that didn't belong to me, freeing me up to own the things that did–I must say, that was a full-time job within itself.

I am very thankful for the community of family, friends and wise counsel God sent my way during this time. It took roughly a year to move out from my sister's place. My credit score had taken such a dive there was no way I could qualify for a place on my own. It was a high school friend who saved the day when we met for a brief lunch and she offered to cosign for my apartment, no questions asked. Before I knew it, my daughter and I were moved in and shopping for furniture. I remember thinking these words during this time: *Buckle up, Mama. It's time to put your foot on the accelerator and turn your new place into a home.*

Setbacks and opposition can rob us of our dreams, but only if we allow it. With every challenge there is a chance to grow. The best thing I have ever done was put my faith in God.

As Mothers We Don't Get The Chance To Quit

"Train up a child in the way he should go: and
when he is old, he will not depart from it."
(Proverbs 22:6)

"For me, motherhood is learning about the strengths I didn't
know I had, and dealing with the fears I didn't know existed."
~ Halle Berry

As mothers we do the best we can. My daughter and I had a very close bond. I was her protector and her provider. Every move I made was for her benefit. My sacrifice and hard work secured a future for us. As parents, I believe, we are the most important teachers. I raised my daughter to know the power of God and the authority of His word. I knew being an only child was difficult. Thankfully, she was surrounded by a lot of other children her age who loved her like a sister. She was known as the neighborhood news reporter, April O'Neil (a reference from the popular television show *Teenage Mutant Ninja Turtles*). She had a very inquisitive spirit who enjoyed covering local stories and sharing the town gossip. She was very intelligent, assertive, and resourceful at a young age.

Our favorite pastime was riding bikes to the park and enjoying a picnic lunch. We traveled to Hawaii, to Disneyland, and to see my mom in Philadelphia every chance we got. She enjoyed go kart racing. We enjoyed movie nights and having breakfast at any time of the day. I was the parent who coordinated all of the fun excursions with her friends and was very active in her school—a fact she wasn't too excited about after she turned twelve years old; it wasn't cool anymore. While we had many great times in the years to follow, one of our biggest challenges was my co-parenting relationship with her father. The bitterness of our divorce and our inability to effectively communicate and collaborate on important decisions was tough, painful, confusing, and overwhelming for my daughter. She was stuck in between the two people she loved most in the world. Unfortunately, that would be our story for years to come.

Being a single mom who traveled and worked weekends, managing the needs of my life, my daughter, and my work was very challenging. I am so grateful for family and friends. It truly takes a village. While I put my daughter first, work-life balance was often difficult to achieve. It was tough. I attended most of her basketball games, track meets, gymnastic, and cheerleading competitions, as well as other activities. How I did it, only the Lord knows. I recall traveling back from a business trip to Oregon when I thought I had timed my flight perfectly so I could attend my daughter's track meet, but there was a delay in the connecting flight. When I finally arrived I noticed her talking to her coach and yelled her name. The smile and excitement on her face was picture-perfect and brought chills throughout my body. I took my seat and cheered her on. After the meet I learned she was asking the coach to delay the run a few minutes until I arrived. I was touched, yet a sadness came over me. This balancing act was taking a toll on me. I needed to get a handle on my schedule because I was missing or showing up late to important events in my daughter's life. I was her number one fan and cheering her on was important to me. I knew she needed my support and that there were sacrifices I needed to make. (Oh, and by the way, she placed first in the 400-meter relay that day.)

It was experiences like these that shifted my focus toward my values and what was most important to me–even if it meant changing my career path. To God be the glory. The leadership team at my company truly believed in the importance of employee's personal interests and families. I was able to make adjustments to my work schedule so I could fully support my daughter's interests and activities. I was so relieved!

IT IS GOOD WITHIN MY SOUL

The moment I welcomed my first grandson into the world was magical. It was the start of a new and special relationship of pure joy. My daughter's world was my world, which now included my grandson, but once it was time for them to move out, a new chapter of loneliness and sadness set in. Empty-nester syndrome was real for me. I felt stuck and abandoned. The house became still. Even though I had remarried, was working, and had a lot on my plate, I just couldn't grasp the fact that they were gone. The good news was she wasn't far away, and we continued to spend lots of time creating great memories together. My daughter worked hard and was an amazing, loveable mom. I cherished every moment we spent together.

SHATTERED CRYSTAL BALL

Sometimes things don't go as planned. In the next season of our relationship, things began to change between us. We still communicated, but not as often as I would have liked. The vision I saw in my crystal ball was shattered. I must admit, I was the most broken version of myself during this time. I took the distance personally. There were many years of painful twists and turns, ups and downs, disrespect and deceit, and investments that yielded no return. I wanted to support my daughter and help her with the road map of life, but she resisted me every step along the way. I couldn't reach her. In my mind, she was still my sweet little girl and, in some ways, I refused to see her as the grown woman she had become. I was feeding my need for control, which only caused more problems. It drove a wedge between us, and I was struggling with my faith, trying to believe our relationship would get better. I wasted a lot of energy feeding my fear instead of my faith. I eventually realized I couldn't feed them both, and made the decision to choose God, kept praying and leaning into His strength. I held onto the glimmer of hope that she was taught to walk in faith and the knowledge that God is always in control.

What I know for sure is that children are a gift from God. As moms it is our job to love and raise our children; nurture them, sow seeds in them, teach them life skills, and support them. However, as they get older and become adults, we must give them the freedom to make their own decisions. It's not about us anymore. It is up to them to use their God-given gifts and talents to make their way.

A DIFFERENT APPROACH

Sometimes it takes a new approach to imagine a different future. It was time for me to let go and let God. With a "moving forward" attitude, I learned to live with the past. When I began to manage my emotions in a different way, I began to see different results. I took the blinders off and realized a few key points. Moms and daughters may have different personality types. The battle over power and who is right or wrong can be vicious–this power struggle makes it difficult to communicate peacefully and limits our ability as moms to effectively pass on our power to our daughters. I firmly believe that time heals, and has the power to shape the present and the future if we allow it.

I FOUND MY SUPERPOWER

As moms we love hard and protect hard. We go out of our way to solve our children's problems. We often get caught up in telling people what to do and how to do it. I started having peace with myself when I focused on my faith and maintained healthy boundaries. I stopped apologizing for holding my daughter accountable to being her best self. I set boundaries and adhered to the course. At the end of the day, our children will do what they want to do. I learned the hard way that I am not going to get my way all the time–I can't control anything or anyone–and I had to be okay with that. I often had to be still, shut my mouth, and hum through the pain (a tactic that I borrowed from my mom's playlist). I learned to stop throwing out my unsolicited advice and strong opinions. No more overstepping or intruding. I stopped getting caught up in my ego and feelings. I learned to listen free from judgment. I showed her through my actions that I believed she was capable of handling difficult situations and making tough decisions. God gives our children the hope and power to endure. Sometimes it is their season to learn what they need to learn. I had to learn to stay in my lane, which was difficult to do and absolutely necessary to move our relationship in a different direction. Thank you, Lord! I finally found *my superpower*: **mind my own business.**

As mothers we don't get to quit, but we can change the way we play when we let our love overcome all. I am grateful God continues to show up for my daughter and six grandchildren. They are a vibrant, talented, athletic, creative, and gifted family. God continues to keep them in His care and showers them with His unwavering love, mercy, and grace. God is putting the shattered pieces back together day-by-day. We remain rooted in love!

On The Other Side
Of The Mountain

"And he said unto me, My grace is sufficient for me thee:
for my strength is made perfect in weakness."
(2 Corinthians 12:9)

"It's the rough side of the mountain that's the easiest to climb;
the smooth side doesn't have anything to hang on to."
~ Aretha Franklin

My power button was back on; at least most of the time. I had a new approach to my strut–activating my *Praise the Lord* spirit. Prayer, energy, positive mindset, but most of all, my faith kept me going. Over the next six years, I felt more comfortable and learned to sit with myself and enjoy me. My light was brighter which helped me to find and make my way. Still lots of meditation and reflection. The sneaky emotions of worry, anxiety, pain, and fear would sometimes steal my peace of mind, but I just kept trusting in God knowing that He would take care of me. I woke up in the morning to be the best version of myself everyday. My first conversation was with God through prayer. When I looked at the girl in the mirror with a smile, that girl in the mirror was finally smiling back at me–the girl beyond the eyelashes, whipped hair and glam. I loved to love her regardless.

I had come to realize that yesterday and today will never be the same, and I needed to keep moving forward. I found life and friends outside of the door versus being tucked under the blanket. I realized my brokenness was not the end of my story—God was preparing a testimony of His glory!

I had a very full schedule. My time was spent raising my daughter, being involved in her many activities, enjoying my awesome career, coaching cheerleading, and volunteering in the community. I dated occasionally and met some interesting men along the way. I didn't rule out marrying again, but being single on purpose to get myself together and whole was top of mind for me.

I prepared myself for if and whenever the time would come. I communicated my desires to God in prayer often:

"Dear Heavenly Father, when you send me my next husband, I pray that you send me a husband who is a man of God with a good moral compass. A hard worker who loves, protects, and supports me, who is emotionally stable, and is a good role model for my daughter, who honors me as his wife, and who never does or says anything to disrespect me. I pray he is tall, intelligent, chocolate and sure of himself, and that he learned how to treat women by watching the way his dad treated his mom and other women in his life. I pray that together we create a loving home. Amen."

These were just some of the strands of my prayer request. Not only was I intentional in what I wanted in my future husband, in doing so, I was finite in my prayer request as to what I didn't want so I wouldn't end up with a project, trying to mother a grown man, a freeloader, a part-time lover, an every-so-often booty call to Tyronne, a bully, a womanizer, a weekday lover, a couch warmer, a sheep in wolf's clothing, that man using his mama car to get around—you get the point.

I was going to be patient and guard my heart. I learned the best way to protect your heart from getting broken is not to put your heart out there or get your hopes up in the first place. Number one on your list is you! Think from your head and not between your legs, no matter what game he throws at you. It's a lot of work trying to raise a grown man. Deception is real. Don't let anyone deceive you nor drag you down. Harsh criticism, broken promises, and trampled boundaries will negatively impact your life sooner than you think. All too often we compromise ourselves, refusing to see what we see, making excuses for their shortcomings. Remember to activate your free gift of discernment without second guessing yourself. Run as fast as you can and keep running! Be patient. God will send you the right person for you in due time. God has someone for everyone.

STRANDS OF OUR STORY, THREE YEARS IN THE MAKING

Every once in a while, right in the middle of the storm, God shines His light on you and brings an unimaginable blessing that feels like a fairy tale. Life can be so unpredictable. Fast forward four years, when I met this tall, dark, and handsome gentleman who brought great joy into my life. He hit all the marks on the prayer request. But the one thing I left out in my prayer list was age. While we looked about the same age, he was six years younger! I recall asking God, *what the heck am I supposed to do with this*? It felt as if I was robbing the cradle. Come on, Stella!

Holidays were very rough for me, usually spent tucked under the blanket due to not having my daughter because of the every other year visitation schedule. This particular Christmas was joyful due to a phone call I had with my new friend who was on tour with the US Coast Guard. He had called me on Christmas day, and stood in a phonebooth in Alaska in the freezing temperature for two hours. It made my heart feel some kind of way. Our conversation was so uplifting, was all over the place, and filled with lots of laughter. (I later learned the cost of the call–wow!)

When he returned from being underway for three months, we learned more about one another and enjoyed each other's company. We communicated so much about life, goals, family, and careers. A whirlwind of adventure–so many fun, spontaneous excursions, walks through the park, and retail therapy sessions. He was a praying man of faith! Sundays were spent getting our praise-on at Acts Full Gospel Church–our food for the week. He was my soulmate.

This is how it started, with chills in my heart. I am very outgoing with a great deal of contagious energy, while he is more reserved, yet fun and adventurous. He often told me, "Don't let the smooth taste fool you."

The possibilities and feelings of sharing a life with him were amazing, yet frightened me at the same time. My feelings were all over the place and I was still decluttering the junk in my life. While I shared my feelings with him, I didn't want him to get caught up in the chaos.

We developed an amazing friendship. We were both clear on what we had in mind for an ideal relationship. I loved that he was patient with me and he appreciated that I put my daughter first without compromise. We brought so much laughter and joy to each other's lives. This man, during my difficult times, was the first one who saw me crash, uplifted me and stood by me with hope. I would always tell my friends and family he would make "someone" a good husband, removing myself from the equation. They would always clap back with "Well, tell us who is this someone? And what about you?"

My hang up was his age and my baggage from the past. This didn't stop us from living our best lives. The relationship had obviously moved from friendzone to dating.

Being in the Coast Guard he spent a lot of time underway in different parts of the world. We both had very demanding careers and lives. We often met up in San Diego for a quick dinner which was perfect because the company I worked for at the time had a satellite office in San Diego. Other times, I wouldn't see him for months. We emailed and wrote love letters to each other, but it would take days and sometimes weeks before they arrived. In between tour duties he surprised and delighted me with gifts. I would receive beautiful tropical floral arrangements at work or delivered to my front door. He would also visit the MAC store every so often and send me new releases of vibrant colors of lipstick and lip liner exclusively selected for me by him. The greeting cards were always gentle, well-written, and thought out. The gifts always seemed to arrive at the right time.

One day in a random conversation, unexpectedly he said, "I love you, Sheila."

My body became numb. I was looking for a place to hide, but there was no place to escape. My mind was crazy and confused. I was in love. Although my situation was getting better there was more to do and my daughter needed me more. Jesus take the wheel!

HERE WE GO, BACK TO THE FRIEND ZONE!

Over the next few weeks, we didn't see each other as much and our conversations were good, but not as warm and fuzzy. I continued to pray to God asking Him to give me a sign, but I guess God was still working on it because I wasn't moved one direction or another. We finally got together for dinner and during our conversation he shared that he received orders to go to Ocean City, Maryland or move to Canada because his enlistment was coming to an end. It felt as if he was giving me some kind of ultimatum. Talk about shock and awe!

Wait, huh? I sat there with a stale look on my face and asked him to repeat what he just said. I remember seeing a smirk on his face as he began to share the steps in the transition process. I asked, "What are you going to do?"

"I am seriously considering the offer," he replied.

"Is this when I get the puppy?" I asked.

He laughed. Side note about that: There was a past relationship where he broke up with a girl he was dating and gave her a dog as a farewell gift. I guess it was so she could have something to practice how to love. Just saying!

"Why do you care?" he asked. "You said that you weren't ready for a committed relationship." Then he added, sarcastically, "Oh, and what about your 'I would make *someone* a great husband' comment."

I was speechless. All that kept twirling around in my mind were his words, "What do you expect me to do on this emotional rollercoaster as you swing from relationship to friend zone?" he added. "One minute I'm your man, the next minute I am your best friend."

I was sad, but respected him more for making his limits unquestionably clear. I had fallen in love, but didn't know how to process my feelings.

AN OUT OF BODY EXPERIENCE

We had arranged to take my daughter to Six Flags (which I still call Marine World to this day). I called to see if we were still on and he gave me a very dry "yes," which I did not feed into. When he picked us up, his mood had changed, thankfully, as he was much more bubbly and engaged. We had a great time gallivanting around the park, enjoying the shows, rides, and all the feels. In the midst of the dolphin show, he and I revisited the conversation about Canada. I asked if he had made a decision.

"Yes," he replied.

"Well, what did you decide?" I asked.

"I am going to accept the offer," he replied.

I am not sure what came over me, but I started laughing–hard. When I finally composed myself, I hit him with so many questions, all of which he answered. Then lo and behold he pulled out his relocation paperwork from his back pocket and said "It's time for me to move on."

My nine year old daughter (remember her, little April O'Neil?), who I didn't think was paying attention to our conversation, whispered in my ear and said, "Mom, it sounds like he is dumping you!"

"Bingo!" he exclaimed.

I was numb. I laughed even harder to keep from crying. What a blow! Still praying and trying to sort things out, I kept my composure and stayed in my body until I got home. Before I got out of the car, I asked, "If you move, will I get a key?"

The response I got from his eyes was "Girl, bye!" Instead he said, "No, I don't think so, but you are welcome to come visit whenever you want."

He was leaving for Japan. What a weekend!

PULSE CHECK!

Sorting things out meant thinking about family, my child, if he wanted children, the age gap, my future life. I soon realized it wasn't as difficult as I was making it appear. We both love God. We were sure that we were both on the same page as far as what we wanted in our relationship. He was emotionally stable and loved my daughter and he loved me. This man had already become our protector and security blanket. My family loved him. We were a team. Now about the six year age gap thing–why can't Stella get her groove back? He was loveable, smart, responsible, trustworthy, kind, considerate, adventurous, and steamy. What more could I ask for?

THE MOMENT!

It was a warm Saturday and I had just returned home from cheer coaching. I received a call from Honey who was still on tour in Japan. He was following up on a package that his friend was going to drop off for me. I checked the porch and told him that it had not arrived. Fifteen minutes later he called back and still nothing. He said that if the package wasn't delivered that day, I'd receive it the next day.

Thirty minutes later he called back and told me his friend confirmed it was left on the doormat. I opened the door, no package. I thought maybe it was delivered to my neighbor in error. I looked down to the right, nothing. I looked to the left and saw a pair of shoes.

Frightened, I screamed as loud as I could. I thought someone was hiding to break in or rob me. Trembling, backing up into the house, my eyes scanned the shoes and slowly up the legs while I was still screaming. I looked up more and to my surprise it was Honey. He had taken a mac flight from Japan. I was shaking and smiling as happy tears fell from my eyes. He picked me up and swung me around. The ultimate gift in the box–he was exclusively for *me*!

At the same time, we both shouted, "Let's get married!"

The deal was sealed. *My Rock. His Shuga.*

Love And Marriage

"So ought men to love their wives as their bodies.
He that loveth his wife loveth himself."
(Ephesians 5:28)

"Love makes your soul crawl out from its hiding place."
~ Zora Neale Hurston

After three years of dating and friend zoning, we were happily married in 1999 at the Cliff House in San Francisco, California. 2024 marked our silver anniversary. Together, we have turned our shared visions into a reality–creating more joy and happiness along the way. I can't believe it has been a quarter century. So many great years coupled with external obstacles that tested our faith.

Through it all God made provisions for us to withstand and overcome every challenge that crossed our path. We continue to pray and speak into existence victory over any unknown future barriers that may come our way. I've learned some good stuff over the years that have been tried, tested and true. Meanwhile, I am still growing, learning, loving and laughing. My strength in my marriage comes from these twelve valuable lessons of love and marriage that we've created and discovered along our twenty-eight year journey together.

YOUR POWER. YOUR CHOICE.

Give yourself a chance to heal first! Stepping into any relationship, knowing who you are first minimizes the chances of letting someone else shape, control or define you, particularly in marriage. Equally important is believing in yourself and having the faith in your own capabilities to love and show up for others as well as yourself.

THE PULSE AND THE PLAN

Love and the heart work hand-in-hand. Falling in love is the pulse. Staying in love and seeing the end from the beginning, while living with the desire to finish with the person you started with, is the plan.

1. **LET GOD BE THE ANCHOR OF YOUR MARRIAGE.** As wonderful as love and marriage is, it will never be fulfilling unless you first shower yourselves in God's unlimited love, grace and mercy. With God as your anchor your marriage will never sink. Let it hold the end of the chain and keep you safe and secure to combat the currents in the midst of the storms.

2. **ONE TEAM. ONE DREAM.** Stay in partnership. Pray together. Break bread together. Rest together. Woosah together. Laugh together. Travel together. Share the bed together. Smell the roses together. Evolve together. Win together. Consider the larger purpose of the life you have created together. You are either in or not. Almost is not enough and doesn't count.

3. **MUTUAL SUBMISSION IS KEY.** Mutual submission is key to a successful marriage. Submission is coming

together as a couple. Me, myself and I can sometimes be the greatest downfalls. Mutual submission, however, goes both ways in marriage. It seeks the good in one another. It is always about self-giving love to each other with the husband leading the way serving his wife with sacrifice, compassion and unity, while the wife makes the house a *home*.

4. **COMMUNICATION.** Talk about it. As soon as you start the conversation it will lead to you having a full conversation. Articulate your thoughts clearly. Take those hands off your hips to avoid saying something different from what your mouth is saying in a non-verbal way. Listen actively without judgment, without reaching a conclusion before you know the entire story.

5. **PILLOW TALK.** For the first five years of marriage we did not have a television in our bedroom. It was our way of building on our bond connecting intimately on an emotional and physical level creating romantic memories along the journey. A great release of the day to relax peacefully, reconnect, and chit chat with no distractions. Taking advantage of the moments sharing affection, and attention often resulted in better sleep quality. Let the intimate conversations of pillow talk keep your sensual bond playful, exciting and lively. It's like dating all over again. Imagine that!

6. **PIVOTAL AWKWARD MOMENTS.** It is *we* over *me* in marriage! Train your heart to offer grace and forgiveness instead of leveling criticism and placing blame on each other. Rather than powering up power down. Break the ice and take the time needed to move to a solution. Take care of each other even when the going

gets rough. At the end of the day, I believe the best way to fight any battle is on your knees. Keep praying.

7. **COMPROMISE.** Talk openly about everything. Leave your egos at the door. Don't keep score resurrecting the past. Let the goal and intention always be to settle on an agreement. Sometimes you may have to agree to disagree. Sometimes you may need to put a pin in it or step aside, reset and revisit at a later date to gain more clarity. We learned how to be better partners through compromise. It's give and take!

Note: Compromise shouldn't come at the cost of your happiness. As a team, the two of you should make sure your mutual happiness needs are a priority and never put on the back burner.

8. **HOUSE MEETINGS & LOVE HUDDLES.** Activated eighteen years and holding. We make time to take care of our business together through our "Annual House Meetings." It's another intentional opportunity to get together on one accord to express love, review finances, household/travel/activities, goal setting, and lay it all on the line. Sometimes, the conversations get heated, but our collaborative agenda is developed to keep us on track.

We also enjoy our "Love Huddles" which are a little more relaxed, but equally important way to discuss things as they come up. As crazy as it may seem, these engagement sessions work and are worth the time.

Our daughter was included in our house meetings. She also came prepared with topics to discuss such as any school, activities, and vacation suggestions. It was important for us to keep the lines of communication open between our blended family relationship. It was our dedicated time to openly discuss her fears and frustrations. We gave her a loving platform and encouraged her to use her voice.

Our parenting focus was on the things we had in common and to come together on the areas we differed. We worked out our differences behind the scenes rather than in front of our daughter. We were determined to encourage a growth mindset while paying attention and praising her for her efforts.

9. **KEEP THE FLAMES AFIRE.** Romance is required in marriage. Be affectionate. Prioritize your emotional and physical intimacy. Let the chemistry you had in the beginning live on. Look at each other, make eye contact, hold hands, hug, and sit close together. This may seem small but it is a crucial step in keeping the flames afire. Keep laughing and having fun! While sharing your love language, stay true to yourself. Choose your friends wisely. Be in alignment with your individual goals and dreams. Above all, continue to nurture your own soul.

10. **PAY ATTENTION TO THE SIGNS AND SIGNALS.** There will be lots of seasons, situations and challenges. During these times be quick to pause, check yourself and dig deeper to really get an understanding of what's going on. Pay attention to the signs and what needs to be done in every situation. Navigate through the transition together. Love shouldn't be a tug of war, it's simply about being there for each other.

11. **LEARN AND TEACH.** Live. Love. Learn. Love is a journey. Learn from other couples and be of help to

struggling couples. Keep your door open to be a resource to motivate and inspire others.

12. PRAY ABOUT IT AND FIGHT FOR IT. No need to keep score. Your marriage deserves to enjoy all seasons. Imagine if you don't fight to make your marriage last forever, you will miss the mushy, cozy feelings of winter, or pass over the promise of spring, the sizzling charm of summer, and the fancy frills of fall. Each season can bring on hope and new life in your marriage. Don't give up. Allow your marriage to transform each season with a time of renewal, adventure, and excitement.

Hold Up, Wait A Minute!

"Knowing this, that the trying of
your faith worketh patience."
(James 1:3)

"Don't wait until you've reached your goal to
be proud of yourself. Be proud of every step
you take toward reaching that goal."
~ Simone Biles

I crossed the finished line. I am officially retired and ready to start this new chapter of my life with a clear sense of purpose; focusing on what is important to me. I am ever so grateful for the abundance of life–starting my day with daily affirmations speaking truth and power to that girl in the mirror. And at the same time, I feel like a fish out of water. Let's do this! I'm ready for all of the fun things retirement has to offer!

Not so fast. Hold up, wait a minute.

Three months after retiring I had rotator cuff surgery on my right shoulder and the ouch was, and still is, real. God sure does have a way of sitting you down. It was time for me to be still and enjoy the comfort of me. My honey was there massaging my arm and assisting me with everything–I mean everything! How does one reprogram their routine from being on-the-go, non-stop action for forty years? What a change from getting dolled up for the day and the activities of daily living in the grind. I now had this pain and arm restriction that was driving me nuts. While grateful that it was a successful surgery, months later I still had limited range of motion, I couldn't comb my hair, prickly gray hairs were beginning to sprout up around the edges, and my armpits needed a shave. Everything felt like a hot mess and was nerve wracking to say the least. Flashbacks of the long and lonely days of the pandemic. Back to the days of comfy clothing, sweats and leggings, strapless everything. *Can I just get a tank top over my head, please?* Thanks to my honey, aka Chef, the one constant was the clanking symphony of pots and pans every morning.

I kept having this feeling that my life was on hold and frantically waiting for the moment when I would actually start living. I was feeling so anxious and impatient coupled with a little crazy. Everything and everyone around me was moving except me. It felt so boring and bleak. I watched the days go by thinking about all the things I could have done. Instead I was wasting my time feeling isolated and not in the mood to take on the day, let alone company. I was absent from myself. On the outside, no one seemed to notice I was falling apart on the inside except me. When we are strong no one seems to notice. We assume the strong person doesn't need help because they appear to have it all together and nothing phases them. But strong people need help too! What changed these experiences is when I realized there were two ways that this story would end. I could either shut down and give it all up, or I could keep moving and keep breathing.

TAKE IT UP WITH GOD

I finally got tired of waiting on how to thrive when I was feeling stuck. I had to lean into my patience and continue to pray. I took a pause and a step back to acknowledge my feelings and the reality of my situation without sugar coating or minimizing the circumstances. It was time to reconnect with myself and reflect, accept, and embrace my current status. The sweet spot of doing me. No alarm clocks, no rush hour traffic, no more commute through the Altamont pass, no more working around the clock, no more sleepless nights, no more endless emails, and no more balancing acts. God has been arranging things in ways I least expected, starting with positive self-talk. *I can do what I want to do, when I want to do it.*

I snapped out of it. My life isn't on hold. I am retired and healing from surgery.

BE STILL, REST, AND ENJOY THE MOMENTS

It was truly a new season of being still and moving to a new level of trust in God. I waited on the Lord in a way that filled my spirit with hope and the strength to carry on and live full even when I was feeling stuck. This meant being still, resting, and enjoying the moments, which was very difficult to do. My days became brighter. While I wasn't very mobile, there was a lot I could do to reignite my spirit. It was time to establish a new routine to support being my best self. Time to start enjoying and doing the things I hadn't had the time to do in a long while. I began walking three miles a day. I began adding color to my diet, sitting down to enjoy every bit of my meals versus having rushed meals on the go. Giving to my favorite charities, enjoying Woosah moments, putting on my sassy hats and attending church, chit chatting with my mom and dad, spending time with my daughter and grands, finishing books from my book club, mini excursions with my Rock, enjoying lunch and laughter with friends, and revisiting fragile relationships in efforts to forgive and let go.

One of the things that has changed as I am getting older is how much more I enjoy spending time with the people I love and allow me to be me. I find great joy in playing my music loud, dancing and being the life of my own epic party. My new love language consists of three letters: F.U.N! I am embracing my whole self, all my imperfections included.

No more nonsense! Out with the old and in with the new. I have more years behind me than ahead of me. I am excited about starting a new chapter in life–making the shift into its own exploration, discovery, and adventure. In the chapters ahead, I am raising my hand for me and letting the words that flow from my mouth move my heart with gratitude, love, intention, and action.

Starting with the first remarkable action of writing and introducing the world to this book, *Strands of Faith: Conditioned by Courage, Hope and Self-Love*. A seed that was planted twelve years ago.

God Knows The Story Behind Your Tears

"Trust in the Lord with all thine heart; and lean
not unto thine own understanding. In all thy ways
acknowledge him, and he shall direct thy paths."
(Proverbs 3:5-6)

"Challenges make you discover things about
yourself that you never knew."
~ Cicely Tyson

Open your heart and feel God's love. Life is tough and so are you. When someone does something hateful, hurtful, or disappoints us, we may never know the motives or situations behind their behavior. We do, however, know God sees everything, and through His power we win when we trust in Him. The pain of relationships ending is real. It can be messy, especially when it comes to our emotions, which can cripple us to our core.

God will help you release those hurtful thoughts and feelings, and will fill that space with joy. God takes our messes and turns them into miracles. It is important to understand that healing is a process. Don't stay in the pit too long. Be kind to yourself while facing the reality of your situation. Call on the Lord to help. Trust Him to be the light in your darkness. He will show up and show out. God will restore and heal your heart. He is always there and enough for you. God will never leave you, nor forsake you.

"A merry heart doeth good like a medicine;
but a broken spirit drieth the bones."
(Proverbs 17:22)

Reinforce the belief in yourself. Get ready to start a new chapter, a journey filled with happiness, adventure and self-love. God knows the story behind your tears. I can bear witness that on the other side of those tears will be joy! Embrace where you are emotionally, and don't give up!

★ Be intentional and specific in your prayer request.
★ It's okay to *not* be okay. It is also *okay* to be okay.
★ Call out each emotion honestly, consider journaling or mediating to help you work out your truth.
★ Do something you used to do. Make time to reconnect with what brought you peace, joy, or inspiration prior to the difficulty.
★ Make time each day to nurture yourself by spending time with loving, positive family members and friends who care about you.

I Am. I Can. I Will.

"Looking unto Jesus the author and finisher of our faith; who for the joy that was set before him endured the cross,..."
(Hebrews 12:2)

"My daily challenge to myself is to be part of "the solution, to be a joyful warrior in the battle to come."
~ Kamala Harris

I AM who I am.
I CAN do all things through Christ who strengthens me.
I WILL carry my own cross to the end.

Let the confetti fall!

When you carry your own cross you put your trust fully in God through the storms and struggles in your life. In spite of the fact that you may be in an extremely challenging or painful situation, you can always trust that God is with you in the midst of your pain.

Afterword

WHAT WILL MY LEGACY BE?

Will it be an overwhelmed, distracted wife, mother, and friend who can't slow down long enough to get one solid thing done? A distraught soul running on fumes, who finds time to focus her energy on everyone and everything else but herself? Will that pushy, wild woman be who they remember? Will it be a nostalgic, old, tired woman with beauty who lives in the past with a flimsy strut?

LEGACY FORECASTED!

I hope and pray that my legacy will be memories of a life well-lived and laughter shared. My prayer life, unconditional love and unwavering faith points others to God. Passing down life memories of family tradition to my daughter and grandchildren of love and respect. Leaving a legacy of love in every life I've touched through God's fruit of the spirit!

Acknowledgements

Many thanks to the following amazing people for being so supportive during the writing of *Strands of Faith: Conditioned by Courage, Hope and Self-Love*

First and foremost, I would like to give praise and glory to **God** for his unwavering grace and mercy.

Editor, **Heather Everett** who graciously kept me excited about writing and was a great caretaker of my message.

Illustrator, **Christine Reite** who beautifully crafted the vision living inside my head.

Photographer, **Eli Pitta** who magically captures my energy and essence through his lens.

Professional Support, **Carla Hilliard** who helped me navigate through the lessons of the workplace.

Blessings, **Father Young** whose enthusiasm about God's message and power verses reinforced the intention of this book.

Trusted first readers of this book **Ali Hall** and **Kimberly "Kimmiko" Keeton**.

Author Endorsements by **Kimberly Endozie, Roberta Gonzales, and Lea Leonardo.**

Worthy Wise Counsel, **Carrie Bratton, Charlotte Hardy, Gwen Johnson, Betty Tatum, Johnnie Mae Tatum,** (Rest in Heavenly Peace, **Shirley Dillon, Ada Howard, Betty Strayhand**).

Confidant/Support Team (aka My Memory Joggers), **Vicki Brown** and **Cynthia Chambers.**

My Dearly Loved Mother and Father, **Sue Tolliver** and **David Terry** who never stopped believing that I would write this book.

My Loving Husband and Best Friend, **Van Young.**

And special thanks to **ME** for having the courage and faith to carry forward my twelve year dream.

Strands of Faith
Book Club Experience

1. From the list below, select three chapters to glean from and pitch to your book club.
2. Work together or form smaller groups and have everyone share a struggle or strand of inspiration based on the chosen chapter and to discuss together the outcomes and possibilities.
3. On your own consider journaling or meditating to reflect on the wisdom that was shared and how it aligns with your personal truth.

Gratitude: What's a hard lesson you were grateful to learn? What are you taking for granted that you can be grateful for? Do you typically think you have more than you need, less than you need, or exactly what you need?

Prayer is a Lifestyle: Why is prayer important in your life? What are the different reasons we *pray* to God? Would you say that prayer is easy or hard? Describe a time when God answered an important prayer in your life. How did the way God answered your prayer affect your relationship with Him?

Worthy Wise Counsel: Tell us about the women who speak truth in your life, someone who believes in you and has a track record of real life experiences. What drew you to these experiences? What is your typical response to advice given to you? Do you accept it gladly? How and where do you find inspiration? How do you pour inspiration into other women?

When We Fumble and Fall, We Rise: Recall a time when you messed up, faced a challenge, setback or failure. How did you react and find the strength to move forward? How did you bounce back? How did you learn to embrace risk-taking and step out on faith? How do you embrace your imperfections?

Make Your Limits Unquestionably Clear: Do you have different boundaries with a friend than with a partner? How do you communicate your *boundaries* and maintain them with those around you? ·

Workplace Wisdom: As you think about your career journey, what actions and activities make you feel purposeful? When it comes to ethics on the job, where does your responsibility to your employer end and your responsibility to God begin? What's the best thing you've ever achieved in the workplace? What is one thing that's been challenging for you recently? What actions are you taking to overcome the challenge? In what ways do you bring wisdom to the workplace?

The Gift of Discernment: What do you find most helpful about discernment? What ways do you activate the gift of discernment in your life? Can you identify an instance in your life when unsound thinking resulted in compromising your intuition?

My Black 6.2: Why is it hard to discuss race? How do you eliminate bias behavior from your daily walk of life? Why do you think code-switching exists? How do you think code switching affects a person's identity? How would you react if someone touched your hair without permission?

Forgiveness Is For You: What does it mean to say "forgiveness is a way of life"? What physical feelings do you experience when someone does something to you that requires your forgiveness? How do you release those feelings?

Woosah Moments: What activities or images come to mind when you think about self-care? What does unconditional self-love look like for you on a daily basis? What prevents you from making time for you? What steps can you take to make time for you?

As Mothers We Don't Get The Chance to Quit: Reflect back on your childhood and the people who made you feel loved. What are some of the things they said or did? What strategies do you use to adapt to your children's unique needs while considering factors like cultural influences and individual circumstances?

God Knows The Story Behind Your Tears: How do you find your "why" in the mist of pain and storms in your life? How do you find courage and hope to endure? Are you speaking your requests into existence and being specific in your prayer request? Provide some examples of how you nurture your mind, body and soul?

What's one thing you learned about yourself?
Share your favorite quote or Strand of
Inspiration @divadazzlestrut

Play It Loud 6.2 Playlist

Scan the QR code below.
Play it loud and let the music vibrate
through your body and move you!

Printed in the United States
by Baker & Taylor Publisher Services